THE

INCREDIBLE JOURNEY

Catherine Martin started life in 1848 as Catherine Edith Macaulay. She was born on the Isle of Skye and later taken to Australia as a child by her father. She worked as a journalist in Adelaide and then as a clerk in the Education Department. In 1882 she married Frederick Martin, who died in 1909. She died in Adelaide in 1937.

The anonymous publication in 1890 of her novel *An Australian Girl*, to be published by Pandora in Autumn 1987, attracted considerable attention; she also published a serial, *Bohemian Born*, which was never printed in book form.

Margaret Allen is a lecturer in Women's Studies and History at the South Australian College of Advanced Education. A keen buyer and avid reader of old books, she developed an interest in early Australian women writers when she was raising a family. She is now researching in this area with particular emphasis on the life and works of Catherine Martin.

AUSTRALIAN WOMEN WRITERS:
THE LITERARY HERITAGE

AUSTRALIAN WOMEN WRITERS
The Literary Heritage

General Editor: Dale Spender
Consultant: Elizabeth Webby

Pandora is reprinting a selection of nineteenth- and early twentieth-century novels written by Australian women. To accompany these finds from Australia's literary heritage there will be three brand-new non-fiction works, surveying Australian women writers past and present, including a handy bibliographical guide to fill in the background to the novels and their authors.

The first four novels in the series are:

A Marked Man: Some Episodes in His Life (1891) by Ada Cambridge
Introduced by Debra Adelaide

The Bond of Wedlock (1887) by Rosa Praed
Introduced by Lynne Spender

Lady Bridget in the Never-Never Land (1915)
Introduced by Pam Gilbert

The Incredible Journey (1923) by Catherine Martin
Introduced by Margaret Allen

And forthcoming in Autumn 1987:

Uncle Piper of Piper's Hill (1889) by Tasma

Outlaw and Lawmaker (1893) by Rosa Praed

An Australian Girl (1894) by Catherine Martin

Three companion books to this exciting new series will be published in 1987 and 1988:

Australian Women Writers: The First Two Hundred Years
by Dale Spender

A lively and provocative overview history of the literary scene and the position of women writers in Australia which shows that any image of the country as a cultural desert was not based on the achievement of Barbara Baynton, Ada Cambridge, Dymphna Cusack, Eleanor Dark, Katherine Susannah Pritchard, Christina Stead and the many other women who have enjoyed tremendous international success.

Australian Women Writers: The Contemporary Scene
by Pam Gilbert

There are a number of outstanding contemporary women writers about whom relatively little is known. This book fills that gap with a comprehensive discussion of the work of Jean Bedford, Blanche d'Alpuget, Helen Garner, Beverley Farmer, Elizabeth Jolley, Olga Masters, Fay Zwicky, Patricia Wrightson and Jessica Anderson.

Australian Women Writers: A Bibliographical Guide
by Debra Adelaide

Covering over 200 Australian women writers, this invaluable sourcebook outlines their lives and works and puts rare manuscript collections throughout Australia on the literary map for the first time. A comprehensive guide to the articles and books written about these women is also included.

THE INCREDIBLE JOURNEY

CATHERINE MARTIN

Introduced by Margaret Allen

London, Sydney and New York

This edition first published in 1987
by Pandora Press (Routledge & Kegan Paul Ltd)
11 New Fetter Lane, London EC4P 4EE

Published in Australia by
Routledge & Kegan Paul
c/o Methuen Law Book Co.
44 Waterloo Road, North
Ryde, NSW 2113

Published in the USA by
Routledge & Kegan Paul Inc.
in association with Methuen Inc.
29 West 35th St., New York, NY10001

Set in 10/11½ point Ehrhardt
by Columns of Reading
and printed in the British Isles
by The Guernsey Press Co Ltd
Guernsey, Channel Islands

British Library Cataloguing in Publication Data

Martin, Catherine
The incredible journey. – (Australian women
writers)
I. Title II. Series
823[F] PR9619.3.M277/

ISBN 0-86358-130-7

CONTENTS

INTRODUCTION

This book, which was first published in 1923, was written by the then seventy-six-year-old writer, Catherine Edith Macauley Martin. Although Catherine Martin had published three novels, a book of poetry, a book of essays as well as various newspaper serials between 1872 and 1923, her work has been largely forgotten and neglected. Until very recently, little has been known of the details of Catherine Martin's life. Few of her papers and letters remain, and this has made more difficult the task of understanding the writings of this elusive figure in the context of her life, her own experiences and reflections. She and her work, like that of so many other women writers, has largely disappeared from view.

However, we do know that Martin was born Catherine Edith Macauley Mackay, c.1848 on Skye, the seventh child of Samuel Nicholson Mackay, crofter, and his wife Janet, née Mackinnon. When Catherine was seven, the family emigrated to the young colony of South Australia with the assistance of the Highland and Island Emigration Society. Described by the authorities as 'poor but very eligible', the Mackay family was one of the many Scots families, dispossessed by the Highland clearances and impoverished by the potato famine, who were forced to emigrate in this period.

In South Australia, the family lived in Naracoorte in the South-East and it is likely that family members worked for wealthy pastoralists, who were developing the country so recently forcibly taken from the aboriginal people. The area was the traditional land of the Bunganditj, the Meintangk and the Marditjali people. As the land was taken from the aborigines there were violent clashes, and the aborigines, losing the economic and spiritual basis of their life-style, were reduced to receiving handouts of rations and blankets from the whites. A missionary, Mrs Smith wrote of the Bundanditj (Boandik) in 1880,

> This once numerous and powerful tribe of South-Eastern natives is now represented by a miserable remnant, which will in a few years, with other aboriginal people of Southern Australia, have withered away before the new mode of life forced upon them by the advent of European colonists in their midst, assisted too often by the cruelties practised upon them by the early settlers.[1]

As no autobiographical writings by Catherine Martin have been located, it is not possible to know how closely she witnessed the dispossession and destruction of the aboriginal people.

Growing up in this rural environment, Catherine Martin, by some means unknown, gained a good education including a knowledge of German language and literature. By the early 1870s she and her sister, Mary, were running a school in nearby Mount Gambier. Keeping a school was of course the means whereby many nineteenth-century women tried to maintain or attain middle-class status while being economically independent.

From at least 1872 Catherine Martin's poetry and translations of German poetry were published in the local press. In 1874 she published her first book, a selection of poems and some translations, *The Explorers and other poems*. Moving to the capital, Adelaide, in 1875, she tried to support herself from her writings published in various newspapers. Failing in this she became a clerk in the Education Department in 1877. Here she was discriminated against financially and failed to gain a permanent position. She was dismissed in 1885. In Adelaide she appears to have found a circle of friends with similar intellectual interests. She met the writer, Catherine Helen Spence and became a friend of the Unitarian Martin family. In 1882, she married Frederick Martin, an accountant.

In the following years the Martins lived in various places, including the seaside township of Glenelg and the remote mining township of Waukaringa in South Australia. They travelled abroad spending long periods on the Continent. In 1890 Catherine published anonymously *An Australian Girl* which was well received in Australia and reprinted the following year. In 1892 she published *The Silent Sea*, under the pseudonym 'Mrs Alick MacLeod'. In 1906, under the name 'Ishbel' she published *The Old Roof Tree*. There is no complete list of her works and it is likely that many still lie undiscovered in old newspapers.

After Frederick's death in 1909, Catherine Martin continued her rather peripatetic life-style, making her last trip to Europe in the years 1928 to 1932, when she was in her eighties. She died in Adelaide in 1937.

The Incredible Journey was published seventeen years after *The Old Roof Tree*. In *The Incredible Journey*, Catherine Martin explored the situation of the Aboriginal people, their culture, their dispossession and in particular, the white practice of taking aboriginal children from their parents. In her earlier works she had discussed the aborigines, their legends, their social customs and the cruelty meted out to them. Among white Australians, the aborigines and their way of life were seen as backward and uncivilized. Martin was a writer who, 'sensed the rich, often gentle world of Aboriginal mythology'.[2] Her approach was one of cultural relativism. Thus in *An Australian Girl*, the central character, Stella, criticized missionaries who lived among the aborigines, but who did not take any interest in their myths, legends and customs. Catherine Martin includes a number of stories of the aboriginal people, making comparisons between these stories and those of other cultures. Thus, after relating a story of the pelicans and the barracoota, Stella commented, 'You see, Australian myths have this in common with those of classic Greece, that they also endeavour to give an account of the origin of things.'[3]

In her earlier works, Catherine Martin touches on issues relating to aborigines and includes some small incidents concerning them. However, they are rather incidental and peripheral to the main concerns of these early works. In her last work, *The Incredible Journey*, the search by Iliapa the aboriginal woman for her son, stolen away by a white man, is the central focus. Aboriginal people are central to the work and their characters and their situations are more fully realized than those of the whites, who are rather shadowy figures.

Speculating about Catherine Martin's reasons for writing this book, one is struck by the coincidence that the book was published just as the South Australian Parliament passed new legislation titled for 'The Better Protection, Care and Control of Aboriginal Children'. This Act increased the state's power over aboriginal children. E.N. Kropinyeri, an aboriginal, commented in a protest letter that the Act legalized . . . 'the Act of taking away the children from their parents.'[4] We do not know whether Catherine Martin was involved in the discussion concerning the legislation, and whether she intended this book as a shot in that debate.

Nor do we know what contact Catherine Martin had with the Arunta (Aranda) people among whom the story is set. She may have seen aboriginal people living on pastoral stations when she visited her brothers' stations in Western Australia. She was an inveterate traveller, but we have no evidence that she travelled through the traditional lands of the Arunta in the far north of South Australia. It is possible that she wrote the book, drawing upon her knowledge of the aborigines and their dispossession by the white occupation of the South-East of South Australia, and of Western Australia, as well as her reading of Australian anthropology.

While we may speculate that Martin wrote this book as a protest against government policy relating to aboriginal children, this is not the explanation she gave. Rather she wrote, 'But frankly, the sole motive of my little book is to put on record, as faithfully as possible, the heroic love and devotion of a black woman when robbed of her child.' She notes that Iliapa's was a true story which 'clung obstinately to my mind as one that must be told'. In deciding to write this story Martin acknowledges the influence of her own mother.

> . . . who, so far from looking on the Blacks as outcasts or untouchables treated them with the unfailing kindness of a gentlewoman, in contact with lowly and very destitute kinsfolk, many of them with estimable and even lovable qualities.
>
> To shirk the trouble of recording the story – though it might quite probably evoke but scant enthusiasm – felt like a sort of treachery.

The Incredible Journey was, for its time, a sympathetic look at the aboriginal people which encouraged the reader to identify with the aborigines, the main figures in the story. The book, however, contains a number of contradictory elements. While Catherine Martin makes Iliapa the central character and reveals the injustices which aborigines suffered at the hands of the whites, she still appears to pay obeisance to contemporary racist ideas about the aborigines. Thus in writing, ' . . . the Australian aborigines are fast dying, and when they have vanished, their passing will form but a minute entry in the record of extinct races.' she was expressing the commonly held belief, sustained by theories of Social Darwinism and by practices of genocide, that the aborigines would inevitably 'die out'. In some of her statements such as, ' . . . black men, who, in some instances show a close resemblance to that prehistoric type known as Neanderthal,' she echoes the Social Darwinist ideas, so powerful in the early twentieth century. However, when she continues this with the observation, ' . . . yet philologists attest that in brain capacity it is little below that of the average European,' she challenges the white assumption of absolute intellectual supremacy.

Throughout the book there are a number of such contradictory elements. In the introduction, she looks at the history of white Australia, praising and even celebrating the spread of the white frontier and the economic development that followed it. Nevertheless, she notes the rather spurious basis upon which the white ownership of the land rests. Discussing the transaction in which John Batman 'bought' the land on which Melbourne stands she wrote,

> Nothing in *opera bouffe* can be richer in comedy than this treaty, the wierd hieroglyphics standing for the signature of Jagajaga, Cololoock and Bugbarie, neither side to the bargain understanding a word the other spoke.

About the proclamation of white South Australia, she commented, 'Not even the customary string of beads seem to have changed hands on this occasion.'

Catherine Martin draws a positive picture of the aborigines. She shows them as a series of individuals with different individual characteristics. She shows them as autonomous and determining people who decide how much they want to be involved with the white ways and the white people. She shows them rejecting white ways, for example, the regular work pattern and European schooling, for their own valid reasons. She also shows aboriginal society breaking down under pressure from white society.

Martin points out that the 'finer traits' of the aborigines had been mis-judged by white society. She compares the devotion of Iliapa in going to find her son, to ' . . . a self-less devotion akin to that of Saints'. By revealing the nobility and saint-like actions of Iliapa, Catherine Martin was challenging the contemporary view of aborigines' lower natures. The device of using the mother to seek her child can also be seen as an attempt to win sympathy and support for the aborigines.

It is interesting to speculate about the reasons for the conflicting elements within the book. Fundamentally they flow from the condition of being European in Australia. Catherine Martin was aware of the genocide and cultural destruction which the white occupation had brought to the Aboriginal people, but like white Australians today, she was also a beneficiary of what the European pioneers had done in taking and developing the country. It can be argued that there are further reasons for these internal conflicts. Catherine Martin knew that the Australian public was extremely hostile to the claims and interests of the aboriginal people. She knew that the book was likely to be met 'with scant enthusiasm'. Given this, she may have moderated the tone of the book in order to make it more acceptable to contemporary white Australia. The book was not as hard-hitting and uncompromising as it could have been in its discussion of the relationship between aborigines and police, and of the taking of aboriginal children from their parents. It was not a matter of one bad white man and a bad policeman as she suggests in the story, but of a system which legitimated the taking of aboriginal children from their families.

Nevertheless, *The Incredible Journey* is an important book, worthy of much more notice and study than it has hitherto received. Katherine Susannah Prichard's *Coonardoo*, published in 1929, has often been described as the first Australian work to sympathetically and fully realise an aborigine as a central character. *Coonardoo* is a more powerful work in that Prichard tackles head-on the issue of sexual relationships between white men and aboriginal women, an issue with which Martin fails to engage. The neglect of this issue, may be explained by the fact that by the 1920s, Catherine Martin, a woman in her late seventies, was a writer from an earlier, more prim era.

Despite her neglect of this issue, Catherine Martin's *The Incredible Journey* is worthy of further study and it, rather than *Coonardoo* should be seen as the first Australian literary work to create an aboriginal protagonist with whom the reader can identify.

Margaret Allen

REFERENCES

1 Mrs Smith (sic) (1880), *The Boandik Tribe of South Australian Aborigines: A Sketch of their Habits, Customs, Legends and Languages*, Adelaide, Government Printer.

2 Healy, J.J. (1978), *Literature and the Aborigine in Australia*, p.229, University of Queensland.

3 Martin, C. (1891) *An Australian Girl*, p.68, Bentley, London.

4 Kropinyeri, E.N. Letter to editor, *The Register* (Adelaide), 21 December 1923.

AUTHOR'S INTRODUCTION TO THE FIRST EDITION

Australia, that unique continent with its queer monotremes and marsupials, has been colonized by two races at eras infinitely remote one from the other. The first comers were black men, who, in some instances, show a close resemblance to that prehistoric type known as the Neanderthal. Though the skull is so ape-like, yet philologists attest that in brain capacity it is little below that of the average European. The Australian aborigines are held to be of Asiatic (pre-Dravidian) origin. But from what centre they came, what ancient race dispersal led to their migration, and in what kind of craft they faced the formidable barriers that separated the old home from the new, no one can say. But they arrived, and their dogs with them. Whether, in the absence of pressure from other intruders, they stagnated below their earlier condition, whether they advanced in some respects, and retrograded in others, are questions wrapped in the mystery that shrouds so much of our wonderful world.

The next migration to the continent was of a more dubious kind. A *Volkerwanderung*, even of the most primitive sort, is part of the trend of human history. But in the convict settlement of New South Wales we have the spectacle of a people disposing of a deplorably unfortunate section of their citizens, under conditions that were morally hopeless. 'In point of expense, no cheaper mode of disposing of the convicts could be found,' was the consideration that weighed with Pitt in deciding on a Penal settlement at the Antipodes. This detachment from ethical responsibility for masses of the nation broken on the wheel of adversity is exemplified also in the utterance of another great statesman of the epoch. 'The bulk of people must labour to gain what by labour can be obtained,' wrote Edmund Burke, 'and when they find success disproportioned to endeavour, they must be taught their consolation in the final proportions of eternal justice.' There is a queer fascination in speculating how far consolations postponed to eternity would have sustained the eminent writer, if the pinch of his own life had reached the pangs of hunger. In the cause of liberty Burke held that Britain was the tutelary angel of the human race. It would seem that one of the gifts of the tutelary angel was the liberty to starve. Such an attitude on the part of those in power may have been an element in making the British people pre-eminent as colonizers.

After New South Wales was transformed into a Colony, free settlers came to Australia in ever-increasing numbers. The site of Melbourne was first occupied in 1835. In the Public Library of that city there is a document in which aboriginal chiefs – so called – make over to John Bateman in return for blankets, food, beads, etc., about half a million acres of land. Nothing in *opéra bouffe* can be richer in comedy than this treaty, with weird hieroglyphics standing for the signature of Jagajaga, Coloolock and Bubgarie, neither side to the bargain understanding a word the other spoke. A year later South Australia was proclaimed a British Colony under the Wakefield system. Not even the customary strings of beads seem to have changed hands on this occasion. A young Australian artist once drew a suggestive sketch of the scene. The new arrivals were gathered under the shade of a gum-tree, taking formal possession of the land. At a distance from them, some aborigines were huddled behind a ridge of sand near the sea-shore, where one of the Old Men of the tribe was supposed to make a short speech, that was transcribed on the margin of the sketch. 'My inside is turned into water. They look as if they had come to stay. This country belongs to us. Here we have the right to walk about, to fish and to hunt; to say when the grass should be burned, and when the animals and the birds of the air should be killed. What will they give us, if they take all this?' Poor old man! He and his were gradually to learn that 'all this' was taken over by the newcomers, in the spirit of the Highlander who, when charged with taking a cow not his own, maintained that he did not steal the animal but took her in the sight of all men as his own.

Queensland, the most extensive, and in some respects the most richly endowed of the States, came into independent existence in 1859.

As the new arrivals gradually took possession of the coastal region the old inhabitants died off or retreated further inland. Their chief memorials are now found in the Museums of the cities, that have grown to surprising dimensions in a comparatively short period. But the time has gone by for Australians to exult in this. The growth is too reminiscent of the lion-cub that was the pride of the household until it became the terror of the inmates. It may seem strange that such increase in size and importance does so little, even in the largest cities, to stamp out the provincial spirit. Australia, however, is not only removed from contact with the old-world beyond all former precedent, but the elements inseparable from such remoteness are reinforced by the magnitude and singular geography of the continent. Thus each centre has a subtly woven tendency to be its own prime universe, immersed up to the ears in its own affairs. The inevitable prominence of material concerns in a new land make them more absorbingly one-sided. Things of world-wide interest – art, literature, abstract thought – have but a hunted and precarious existence. Men compromised by such matters acquire the reserve of devotees, whose faith is a sort of treason against the great Gospel of 'getting on.' The more ideal pursuits are in the main regarded as exotics, to be treated like the mermaid found on the sea-shore by a Dutchman, who took her home, scraped the sea-weed from her skin, dressed her as a woman of Holland, and set her to spin and to bake bread. Even in the affairs of the market-place, there is often a narrower and more embittered spirit than elsewhere. Workers regard the Capitalist as a greedy and crafty parasite, that should be in some way eliminated from the social system. The Capitalist, on his side, looks on the Labour Party as a sort of heathen fortress, stuck all round with the Christian heads of employers, who have been slain to make a Paradise for working men. But this is too much like embarking on a 'dim and perilous way.' It is better to get out into the country, and go Outback in a leisurely fashion.

Some of the older agricultural districts, with wide wheat fields, varied by vineyards, by orchards and gardens, in their season swathed with mists of delicate blossoms, full of the hum of bees – flocks and herds feeding here and there, have all the charm of scenes immortalized in the idylls of the old world. But the invariable background of trees gives a stamp of its own to the Australian landscape. The woods, too, largely composed of eucalypti, have a more sombre tone than in other lands. The eucalyptus has been acclimatized in so many countries that it now holds its own as a citizen of the world. Yet it is surprising how many remain ignorant of its claims to supreme distinction.

In waterless country it is more like a spectre brooding on life than a living member of the vegetable kingdom. Indeed, in all places habitually dry, the spare form, the meagre foliage, the dull colouring – something in its outlines, as of concentrated detachment from a glancing gaiety – mark the tree as a creature that has kept hold on existence through harrowing destitution. But close to water unvisited by drought, it rivals an English oak in the density of its gracious shade. For one of the most distinctive traits of the tree is its almost human responsiveness to any change of environment. In this it gives support to the belief that plants may be endowed with an instinct akin to consciousness. Each different contact produces some alteration to form, some divergence in the leaves, in the oil-dots, in the colour and veining; some diversity in the arrangement of the unique cup-formed blossom-buds, with closely fitting lids, whose appeal to the French naturalist's imagination led to the beautifully descriptive Greek name. This Protean quality has made the Eucalyptus the despair of classifiers, but to the mere laity such endless variations have a great fascination.

The blossoms of the myrtle order, with a delicious fragrance, as of mingled syringa and wild honey, have more sameness of outline, but great fertility in shades of colour, from waxen white to deep cream, from faint pink to fiery flame. These gradations do not occur in the same soil, not do the various kinds of the tree blossom in the same season. There is probably not a month in the year in which some may not be found somewhere in bloom. The blindness of the early comers to the attractions and qualities of the eucalypti, which most of them lumped together as 'the queer things called gum-trees,' was part of the nostalgia of people who still longed for the old country. Eyes accustomed to the strong – almost metallic – verdure of Northern lands, to the picturesquely rent, cleft, furrowed and scalloped leaves of deciduous trees, could not do justice to the smooth narrow leaf, evasive in its hues of grey-green and grey-blue, ranging in shape from the faint crescent of a moon one night old to the round curve of a reaping hook. A leaf exquisite in its grave simplicity as a lotus bud on the shrine of Gotama. It is as if all the contrasts in the life of European and Australian trees were gathered up in their leaves. Those that slip from their buds in Spring to fall in discoloured clouds in Autumn can well afford to indulge in fantastically ornate edges. But how far other it is with those that often have to face rainless years, to live through droughts that suck the life out of the earth, till it is barren as the sea-shore, bleached and sinister-looking as if overtaken by the fulfilment of the dark prophecy: 'on tree and herb shall a blight descend, and the land shall become a desert.' But through it all the Eucalyptus lives on and on, until once more the rains pour down. Is this capacity of braving the prolonged fury of sunshine, which draws the sap out of every other growth, knit up with the unrivalled properties that make the eucalyptus a tree for the healing of the nations? Not only the oil so mysteriously secreted, but the leaves in their raw state, and the gum or kino, have great medicinal qualities. In fact, many of those best qualified to judge affirm that the hygienic value of the tree is still but partially understood.

Features of great interest in the earlier stages of the journey Outback, are the country towns. With their municipalities, churches, schools and libraries; their annual shows of stock, grain, flowers and vegetables, etc., revealing from season to season the capacities of adjacent districts; their well-conducted newspapers, full of local colour, yet with surprisingly comprehensive epitomes of world news, they form communities that are largely self-governing, and afford many avenues of decent competence. They often have naive survivals of village life, such as an inexhaustible interest in the lives and doings of neighbours, chiefly because they belong to the same Parish. There is too, in some of them, a complete suspension of the mistrust and the intermittent growls that too often mark the intercourse of diverse Sects. If this goodwill among the various denominations could be carried to a basis of union, that would abolish futile divisions, much might be effected for the more isolated regions that now remains undone. An Anglican Bishop, speaking of his Diocese some years ago, said that even in townships of very moderate size, he found five separate houses of prayer, where five very scanty congregations were ministered to, by five underpaid ministers, who rode on five underfed horses, to preach what is substantially the same Gospel.

It may be urged that places of worship so much sterilized by offering bundles of words smeared with honey, in place of the bread of life, are hardly of value enough to make their absence a matter of great importance. But this view is discredited when face to face with far inland Bush townships, whose social relaxations centre in a squalid little public-house, and occasional horse-races, without a single outward witness for man's inner life or better aspirations, save a poor little shack of a school, in which no religious teaching is given. It is surmised that within the limits of man's terrestrial career, we must anticipate changes of belief as fundamental as those that at present separate us from primitive man. But those who crave for the impulse of spiritual life, often look back rather than forward. Though 'gross and obscure mists' have spoiled so much in the past, yet the heart turns to the records of early simple worship, with the longing of a child for a lost home. To the informal meeting together for prayer, the simple address that, at times, breathed the love of God into whole assemblies, the breaking of bread that symbolized the sacredness of human fellowship. . . . Despite all – something of these survive in modern churches. They still cherish ideals of faith and love and hope, to rouse the soul from the torpor of material aims, to bring some release from the common routine of common life. Nowhere in the world are such influences more sorely needed than in lonely little settlements Outback. It has been an unfulfilled dream to found Centres in such places that would combine worship, hospitals and libraries. Something has been done, and though not on these lines, yet it is a hopeful beginning.

In leaving the more settled districts, two great wants are increasingly revealed; the sparseness of population and the lack of means for conserving the rainfall. Though good seasons sometimes come in succession, cradling men in the hope that the hard times have gone for good and all, yet the spectre of drought never really goes away. It has been, and is, the family ghost of innumerable Australian homes. Not until wide-spread and combined action is taken, can the periodical calamities of drought be mitigated, if not overcome. There is alluring hope in the fact that when droughts break up, it is as a rule in a way that seems literal fulfilment of the old promise: 'Prove me now herewith . . . if I will not open you the windows of heaven, and pour you out a blessing, that there shall not be room enough to receive it.' The rivers are flooded, creeks overflow, tanks, dams and reservoirs pour over, native wells are submerged, swamps become lakes, lakes like inland seas; waters not marked on any map, make for a time an appearance of imposing dimensions. Thus from time to time oceans run to waste of the country's most coveted wealth. Much has already been done to serve as an inspiration for future action. Western Australia in a notable instance leads the way. The Mundaring reservoir is capable of holding four thousand million gallons of water. From this is pumped daily, through a steel conduit, five million gallons to the two goldfields of Kalgoorlie and Coolgardie, also to places *en route*. Anyone who has stood at Mundaring, and watched the sheet of surplus water pure and clear, flowing over into the Helena Vale river, carries away an enduring memory of the marvellous feats skill and labour can achieve, in collecting and distributing water to support life, and a great industry in the heart of a desert rich only in gold. But in dealing with the country at large, the conservation of water is one of the many problems that can be solved only with a greatly increased population.

Many elements have conspired to keep back the more rapid peopling of Australia. Chief among these is the determined drift city-wards. It is as if the old pioneering instinct of our race had suffered a serious decline This is possibly an outcome of the industrial era; the multiplication of machinery in all directions inducing a diminution of will power. The automatic quickening of exterior life, tending to restlessness, and the more sensational life of crowds, making country work distasteful, and solitude all but unbearable. It is as if the price paid for the monotonous cunning swiftness of the machine was in part a deadening of the worker's interest and initiative; as if with the ever-growing subjection of the senses to artificial appeals, active intelligence is gradually being bred out of the mass-mind.

But as was said by one of old, it would be a great toil to discuss all particulars – more especially those that are obscured by so many cross currents. Suffice it to say that though a feeling of anxiety has been for some time latent in Australia, because of the ever increasing additions to the parasitic city populations, combined with what, in some directions, has been all but an arrest of settling in the country, yet no effective action was taken to remedy these evils. There was need of some strong impartial influence to overcome the apathy of centres, widely separated, not only by distance, but lack of mutual sympathy. Australians owe a great deal to the distinguished visitor, who has done so much to awaken the general consciousness of their country, to the vital necessity of attracting to it a selected flow of immigration, to possess and develop land that needs only human industry and judicious management to turn it from empty spaces into prosperous homes. To stress the fact that this necessity rests in the last analysis, not alone – not even chiefly – on economic grounds, but on the naked question of race survival, was a masterly appeal to emotions that are the most deeply rooted in a virile nation.[1]

The interest of travel Outback is much increased, when trains are exchanged for a mail-coach or motor. The contact with mother-earth is closer, and in the greater leisure of driving, every aspect of life assumes a new importance. A little township with a garden here and there that has shrubs and bloom in spite of continual heat; a small clearing where a cereal is being nursed into life; men employed in putting up a fence, in droving sheep or cattle, in digging a well, putting down an artesian bore or cleaning out a dam – all have the importance of pushing further the frontier of new development. Even the sounds that tell of human settlement, the bleating of sheep, the lowing of cattle, the meditative tinkle of a camel or bullock bell – above all the fluting voices of children at play near some homestead – have the appeal of the first sparse web of colonizing gradually laying its seal upon the wilderness.

In such remoteness from the ordinary turmoil of affairs, everyday events are often charged with new meaning. Wavering lines of waterfowl, seen in flight against an evening sky, speak of the links that make the whole world kin. They sow not, neither do they gather into barns, but like man they are at times overtaken by the measureless thirst of the desert. They wing their trackless way, to work out their own destiny in some chosen haunt, like the men who by shore and far inland, are the forerunners of future comers; all obeying the wonderful mandates of life – depth behind depth – by which, unconsciously or of set purpose, the toil and hardships of one generation are endured to make the homes or nesting places of the next. . . . But some sights have a glamour that raise the heart above all the traffic of this earth. When the dawn, 'rose red with beatings in it as if alive,' steals into the East, above the silent woods of an unbounded plain, while the stars wane, and the moon withers, it is as if Eternity had dropped into the midst of time, and sorrow had been turned into a tale of derision.

Many of those who blazed the first tracks to the outer regions of

[1]Since these lines were written, the British race at home and abroad has suffered a heavy loss in the death of Lord Northcliffe. One living in a remote part of Australia – native born in the third generation – writes: 'It was many a long week after Lord Northcliffe had "gone west," that the sad news reached us here. . . . Never before in my remembrance has anyone given a message to this country, that has carried so far and wide as his warning on the danger of our empty Continent. . . . He has left us a legacy that cannot perish.'

Australia, are men of marked personality, and have contributed much to the forms of settlement, for which these regions to begin with are fitted. Like poets, pioneers seem to a large extent born with the intuitive qualities that fit them for their career. But instead of living in the world of ideas, and adding to its emotional and spiritual delight, theirs is the sterner task of developing, and carrying on in country under conditions, that to begin with have little correspondence with civilized existence. They and some of their descendants form the most distinct type that Australia has yet produced. Few problems are more fascinating than the growth of national characteristics, or more complex and baffling. The ordinary enquirer as to cause and effect, is soon reduced to the tactics of the Actor-manager, when he said of a costly scene: 'Imagine all this to be done already. We cannot produce a house covered with pearl-embroidered brocade, and a lady in beaten gold.'

But it lies on the surface that Outback is a territory, in which a man cannot make headway without facing issues that probe character to its depths. At close grips with untamed surroundings, that are as destitute of luxuries as a raft in mid-ocean, he is schooled to hardship and self-reliance, to make as light of danger in an emergency as if he were on a battle-field. There are no wastrel, parasitic and servile callings Outback. Almost all are in the open air, worthy of a sane mind in a healthy body – avocations that bear the stamp of man's primeval needs, rather than the mark of Dagon, impressed on so much of the wares that flood the ephemeral markets of furious competition.

It is often a trait of the Outback man, that he can find his way in country quite strange to him, as if he knew it by heart. A faculty that at times seems as clear cut as the instinct of an infant swallow that, a few days out of the shell, cowers with fear in the mother's absence, when a sparrow-hawk hovers above her nest. It seems established that the human race in developing intellect, lost largely on the instinctive side. When this is so curiously active, it is as if drawn near to that formidable heart of nature, where life and death are so closely neighboured, the earlier safeguards were once more called into play.

This may belong to the domain of conjecture, but it is certain that the Outback man is curiously free from that form of self-will which clings to illusions because they are pleasant. He loses the art of veiling the tragic side of life with the evasions that are popular in cities all the world over. The sequence of iron laws, serenely indifferent to human fate, make their own mark on one, who now and again has come upon a scattering of bleached bones and tattered clothing – all that was left of some Pilgrim who took the wrong direction, and was stamped out of existence like a superfluous lizard. Such experiences bred a habit of stripping optimistic theories to the skin, with a ruthlessness that has little in common with the tact of the man, who was said to take down our idols from their pedestals so tenderly, that it seemed like an act of worship.

Not that the Outbacker is at all morose, or prone to impose his own opinions upon others. His latent sense of humour is too strong for that. But he has ridden so many solitary days from sunrise to sunset, that meditation has become a second nature to him, and though he has learned to draw quiet enjoyment from the various aspects of nature and the sparse deposit of events around him, yet there have been few currents in his days to submerge the realities that lie so close to him. When drawn into talk, he speaks from his own knowledge and observation, instead of reflecting borrowed thoughts as a mirror gives back the shadows that cloud its face. . . . Frequently he has the love of books that gives him a refuge in his mind, as one that has roamed in many realms of thought. It is fortunate for our pioneering and adventurous race, that literature – in some ways the most comprehensive and poignantly expressive of all the arts – is the one great gift of the Muses that can be cherished at the most remote outposts, 'giving a forgetfulness of evil, and a truce from care.'

Where an arid region has reached its barest phase, there is no form of agriculture or fruit-growing. Gardens are unknown save on some head station, favoured with an abundant supply of permanent water and a skilful gardener – usually a Chinaman. Townships have dwindled down into a few straggling huts built of iron and rough timber. Now and then tracts of country are seen that are like pictures of the legend in which a god vanishes, taking with him all the known gifts of the earth. There is no landmark, no point of arrival or departure; nothing to cast a shadow at the rising or the setting of the sun. There is no sight or sound of any living creature on the earth or in the air. Yet sometimes in such a waste a strange vision of beauty suddenly transforms the scene: rising high into the air a fountain of artesian water crystal-clear, that as it falls flows away in an enchanting little stream, bordered with verdure and alive with birds. Among these at times are grebes, that have come from a far distance.

Having but very limited powers of flight, it is a problem how they compass such long journeys.

The marvellous effect of water in the midst of sterility explains, in part, how the theory of sympathetic magic for the growth and maintenance of the food supply, has been more thoroughly and elaborately carried into practice by the Tribes of Central Australia, than by any other race in the world. The rituals that they observe with such amazing assiduity have been exhaustively revealed in the invaluable work of Messrs Spencer and Gillen. Though these laborious ceremonies were often manifestly as resultless as more polished beseechings, that two and two should make five, yet the fact that sooner or later the worst drought broke up, and the desolation of death was replaced by an abundance of plants and animals, profoundly established the faith of the Tribes in their traditional magic. It is a significant instance of the way that the order of nature may, in a confused fashion, be apprehended by the primitive mind, though it may never sufficiently evolve to recognize the universal reign of law.

Artesian bores contribute largely to the occupation of the more arid regions Outback. Also the strong natural grasses, the many varieties of the drought-resisting salt-bush, and the tracts of edible scrub that afford valuable reserves of fodder in the vicinity of water-courses and creeks, even when these are quite dry. For in such country sheep and cattle runs form almost the only centres of activity. On many of these Stations, Aborigines may still be found under very tolerable conditions, being to some extent in touch with their old traditions and observances. The routine of work yearly repeated, in the care and breeding of flocks and herds, is soon acquired by the able-bodied natives. When a certain latitude is allowed them – to 'go bush' or on holiday – at such times as station work is least exacting, they are often faithful retainers, year after year. In all the States – save Victoria, the 'cabbage garden' of the Commonwealth, in the sense of being compactly near the coast, with most of its land fit for cultivation – there are far inland squatting districts that owe part of their prosperity to these workers, who are paid in food and clothing. Their dependents are also given a certain quantity of rations. Their women are sometimes employed for domestic work on the Stations, and, as a rule, very kindly treated by the mistress. Something of this is incidentally shown in 'The Incredible Journey.' But frankly, the sole motive of my little book is to put on record, as faithfully as possible, the heroic love and devotion of a black woman when robbed of her child.

It is a commonplace that the significance of a tale does not depend on its being a slice of life. But there are some narratives that would never be written unless they had happened, and this is one of them. It is in the main as related by one who knew the details at first hand. A touching story vividly told bites into the hearer's mind. But in cold type emotion is as if stiffened beyond the reach of words, and words themselves so easily become a series of signs that mock their writer, with a dismayed sense of failing to carry their real message. Yet 'when other petty griefs have done their spite,' impulses remain that make writing on a certain theme a necessity – almost as if apart from the writer's will. Despite the feeling of failure that induced rejection of one version after the other when committed to paper, Iliapa's story clung obstinately to my mind as one that must be told.

It is said that in the beginning magic and words were one. Certainly there are times when words feel like something more than mere symbols of interpretation. Thus it was now and then, a little like a spell, that when Iliapa was put aside, and half forgotten, the memory of an Aboriginal phrase, or a stave from a Corrobboree chant, should suddenly summon her once more into the sunlight. . . . But in reality, the ground-root of this teasing importunity was the influence of a mother who, so far from looking on the Blacks as outcasts or untouchables, treated them with the unfailing kindness of a gentle-woman in contact with lowly and very destitute kinsfolk, many of them with estimable and even lovable qualities. Here was a notable instance establishing a point of view that to many ways almost an offence, or at best an eccentric fad. To shirk the trouble of recording the story – though it might quite probably evoke but scant enthusiasm – felt like a sort of treachery. All the more that the implacable rigours of their native surroundings often made the finer traits of the Australian aborigines seem to the present Masters of their country, but part of the equipment of grotesque figures on a latern slide. Let one instance speak for many.

In an interesting little book written some years ago by an able Australian ornithologist, he relates that having to cross part of an unknown desert, he secured a black fellow as a guide in the matter of native wells. The guide was accompanied by his wife, who was followed by five dogs. She was told that these must be destroyed, or left behind, as no water could be spared for them on the journey. She was carrying all the requisites that even aboriginal needs raise to a considerable load, her man limiting his share to a few weapons. But she would not have her dogs killed or leave them behind to perish. She had a vessel which she filled with water, and carried on her head for more than fifty miles. When the party halted, she would be seen under a bush, giving water to her dumb mates, one after the other out of a jam tin, reserving a little for herself out of the ration. It is all told in the manner of an indifferent spectator, with casual mention of the fact that the black man relieved himself of his weapons now and then by adding them to the woman's burden – apparently with no protest from the victim or the onlookers – certainly with no appreciative word of her unselfishness.

There is no moment of life, in which one is more tempted to regard the career of our race, as a 'discreditable episode in one of the meaner planets,' than when brought into contact with the ill-usage of dumb animals. 'Talk of fame, honour, wealth,' wrote Darwin on one occasion, 'all is dirt compared with kindness.' The kindness of the Aboriginal woman is of peculiar ethical value. Nature so often terrifies us, in the guise of a power that is no more concerned with the good or ill of human creatures, than she is with the subtle device of a serpent's sting, or with the insects that swarm by the million into existence on a tropical night – tiny flames of life lit in the midst of infinity – only to be quenched in a few brief hours, leaving a refuse on the verandahs, of grey and brilliant little corpses in drifting heaps, that touch the heart with an unbearable and haunting pang of kinship. In the presence of such ghastly waste, dark questionings arise as to any beautiful end being set before the world and its inhabitants.

But that a wild woman of the lowliest race which has struggled to the rank of humanity, should, for the sake of her poor despised dogs, add so much to her deadly load, while she panted on half naked for a woeful distance over burning sand – this in a glimmering fashion seems a pledge that Nature has some affinity with good as a development of her order. For the gesture was as beautiful in its way as the Koranaic verse: 'There is no beast on the earth, nor bird which flieth with wings, but the same is a people like unto you. Unto the Lord shall they return.'

Unto the Lord have returned innumerable powers and nations that have been cast upon the dust-heaps of the earth, like the playthings of a wanton child. The Australian aborigines are fast dying, and when they have vanished, their passing will form but a minute entry in the record of extinct races. To those who have ears to hear, it is worth telling, that even among this people there have been those who were in a measure liberated from the thraldom of the lower nature. Iliapa and others have borne witness to this, with a selfless devotion akin to that of Saints, whose relics have been treasured to ward off disease, crime and sudden death.

C.E.M.M.

CHAPTER 1

Though close to the naked heart of Australia, the Jimarra Creek has many spots of great beauty. More especially before the summer has set in with tropical heat and withering hot winds. In mid-October, some years ago, where the Jimarra took a wide bend, and was more like a river than a creek, shady trees, shrubs in blossom, wild flowers, the sound of running water, and the songs of birds, made up a scene that seemed to have gathered together most of the treasure of the Bush. Away to the north, a low range of hills, blue against the bluer sky, marked the beginning of country that was more like the skeleton of a perished world than the kindly earth of living creatures. But in this valley of the Jimarra, there was not a harsh outline, nor a trace of desolation anywhere to be seen. It was a place that made the traveller dream of prosperous homes, surrounded by tilled fields, by teeming gardens and orchards. But though all these belong to the days that are to come, the silence of this perfect afternoon was suddenly broken by the shrill calls and the loud laughing of children. They were black boys and girls, barefooted and bareheaded, with little to cover them beyond the meagre clothing of a station camp with waist-girdles of 'possum skins, and necklets of little shells and bright berries. But the love of a story was just as deeply rooted in their young hearts as if they were arrayed in purple and fine linen. They had been listening for a long time to an old woman called Labea, who was a born story-teller, with an endless stock of tales about everything that was to be seen in the heavens above and on the earth beneath. Sun, moon and stars, lightning, thunder and rain; woods, plains, gullies and swamps – all the creatures that live in them, and the birds that fly in the air – nothing came amiss when the mood was on her, and she had plenty of tobacco to smoke.

Such was the case this time, when Labea poured out the wealth of her memory and invention, ending at last with a very absurd story of a crow, that sent her audience into fits of laughing. In the midst of the merriment, a voice called from a distance in the Arunta tongue – 'Iliapa, Iliapa, I want you.' One of the oldest of the girls at once arose, and called out 'I am coming.' It was her sister Nabata, who was going to look for sugar-bags, as the natives call the honey of the wild bee.

Iliapa was a little more than three years old when her mother died. But she always said she could remember her, and that she often came in dreams.

'I saw her last night,' she said all at once as the two went on by the bank of the Jimarra. Though she mentioned no name, Nabata at once knew that she meant their mother. Sometimes when Iliapa spoke of her dreams, Nabata would pretend not to hear. But now she frowned and said, 'You are a silly girl. You shut your eyes and think of things. Then by and by you say, "Oh, I had such a wonderful dream! I will show you how you dream."'

Nabata stood stock-still, put her hands down by her side, and shut her eyes. Then opening them wide, she said with a look of wonder, 'What do you think I saw?'

'Tell me,' said Iliapa, laughing, for she was always amused by her sister's mimicry.

'Well, I saw three baby moons running after a very old star. One of them tried to run ahead, another ran alongside, and the last sat on the tail of the star.'

'On the tail? As if a star had one like a 'possum.'

'But some have. Only instead of being quite small, the tail of a star spreads over the sky as far as you can see. You have not been long enough under the sky to see a star like that, but I saw one before you were born.'

What Nabata meant was a comet, that had appeared in the sky many nights when she was six years old, a few months before Iliapa saw the light of day. Their father's name was Erungara, and had been at one time known far and near among the Arunta tribe as a very wise medicine man and Oknirabata, or great teacher. A man who knew more than any other the old laws and history, the ancient customs and ceremonies of his people. But a great quarrel broke out between him and the older men of the tribe. This went so far, that one of his enemies attacked him one day when they were alone in the woods, and left him for dead. He lay for some time between life and death. But he was a very strong man and gradually his wounds healed. But though he recovered, his memory at times failed him, and he confused his own thoughts with old tribal customs and beliefs. His enemies made this an excuse for taking all authority from him, and forbidding him to take any part in their secret councils, and the more important ceremonies. But those who were in the camp of the Jimarra Station, as well as many others of the tribe, said that no other medicine man had so much skill, and no other teacher so much knowledge.

It was near sunset when the sisters returned after gathering all the wild honey they could find.

'Perhaps the next time you hunt for sugar-bags, I may not be with you,' said Nabata in a half-mysterious way.

'Where would you be?' asked Iliapa in a tone of surprise.

Nabata laughed, but made no reply. The difference in their years – Nabata was a few months over twenty, Iliapa little more than fourteen – had accustomed the younger to be sometimes treated as if she were still a baby. So she asked no more questions. Yet somehow she felt as if there was more in Nabata's words than merely a love of teasing.

That night she woke up before the dawn had come into the sky. She thought she heard whispering, followed by some movement.

'Nabata,' she called softly, 'are you awake?'

A night-jar screeched in the distance, opossums hissed and chased each other in the gum-tree, above the little ilta, or mia-mia, that the sisters shared in the women's camp. But there was no reply, and Iliapa lying down once more was soon fast asleep.

The next thing she knew was that Labea – the noted teller of stories was their father's sister – stood over her at sunrise asking with a malicious smile:

'Where is Nabata?'

'There in her own corner,' said Iliapa sleepily, pointing to the opposite side of the mia-mia.

'Open your eyes and look well,' cried Labea with a note as of victory in her shrill voice, that made it more piercing than usual. Iliapa, now wide awake, stared at the recess in which Nabata always slept. There was nothing but the huddled remains of an old rug, made of wild-cat skins.

'You are playing some trick on me. Tell me – tell me where she really is.' Iliapa by this time was seriously alarmed, and found it hard to hold back her tears. But she knew if she cried, that her aunt would mock and jeer at her, and keep her all the longer in the dark as to Nabata's absence. 'The next time you hunt for honey, I may not be with you' – these words, as well as Labea's manner, and many whispered talks lately between her aunt and sister, filled her with a kind of terror, that in some way or other, Nabata was lost to her.

Labea, without making any reply, turned over the few things that remained in Nabata's recess.

'Nothing you see of any use,' she said in her thin, harsh voice, that cracked now and then like brittle sticks breaking underfoot. 'Her good rug of 'possum skins, her big netted bag and flat basket, her digging stick and her climbing stick, her pretty necklaces, her long waist-belt of emu feathers, the clothes they gave her when you were at Balkara, all gone.'

'But no evil has come to her, you know where she is,' pleaded Iliapa in a small feeble voice. She had no longer to struggle against tears; her eyes were hot and dry, her heart fluttering like a bird newly caged.

'Yes, I know – and as you are not a cry-baby I will tell you.' Labea stepped to the opening of the mia-mia, and looked for a moment steadily at the sun. 'By this time,' she said, turning to her niece, 'your sister and Opopa have got as far as the Curlew Swamp. Now don't cry out or begin to shake like a leaf in a thunder-storm. Sit down here, and be like your grandmother on the mother's side, who went through fire and water, and walked without eating for two days and a night, till she caught up the one who robbed her, and got back what was stolen. You know that your father promised your sister in marriage when she was a baby at the breast – the same as he has promised you – to a man old enough to be her grandfather. By great good luck this old man was eaten by an alligator, when he was on his way to take Nabata. Well, Opopa of Roalmah came a short time ago, and asked your father to give him Nabata. "No," said your father, "it is against some old rule of the Arunta people."'

'Nabata, are you there?' said one near the opening of the mia-mia.

'That is your father,' said Labea with a chuckle. It was clear she much enjoyed the news that she had to give him. As she turned to go she said to Iliapa, 'Now you curl down there with your little 'possum and stop shaking. When your father is gone, I will bring you some tea and flour bread.'

'You cannot see Nabata just now,' she said to Erungara, who was waiting patiently beside the mia-mia. 'Can I give her a message from you?'

'The message is for you as well,' replied Erungara with a stern look. 'It is known to me that you have been too friendly to Opopa – have even taken Nabata to meet him by the Pool of the Pelicans, when I was away from the camp. Now I have come to tell you and Nabata for the last time, that I cannot give her to Opopa; it would be against some of our old marriage rules.'

Labea's answer to this was to burst into a loud, shrill laugh. There were people who said that when Labea laughed much, it was a sign that some of her friends had trouble. Her looks did not belie this legend. One of her eyes had been put out in a tribal scrimmage. This loss had a weird effect, made more marked by a strip of swan's down bound round her forehead, and tied in a full bow above the vacant socket. Her straggling locks of snow-white hair, falling under this band against her long, thin face, gave her the look of a melancholy and haggard bird of prey, rather savage and ready to snap at the least offence.

When she stopped laughing, Erungara said with grave displeasure, 'You are like a kookaburra in a tree-top, that shrieks and cackles without cause or reason. Tell me where I can find Nabata, so that I may speak to her.'

Labea stood away from the mia-mia, and looked hard towards the south, smiling as she did so, in a way that filled her brother's mind with alarm.

'Why are you looking so far away,' he asked, 'as if Nabata were at some great distance?'

'Your thought is true. By this time she is a long shadow beyond Curlew Creek,' said Labea slowly, as if each word were wild honey on her lips.

Erungara glared at her for some minutes without moving or saying a word. Then he sprang to her side, and caught her by the right arm, gripping it so tightly that she gave a little scream.

'Are you telling the truth? Has Nabata really gone away with Opopa? Did you know she was going?'

'Let go my arm or I will tell you nothing,' cried Labea in a very angry tone. Erungara let her go, for he knew of old that Labea had a fiery temper and that nothing was to be got from her by force. She rubbed her arm, looking fiercely at her brother.

'I have a good mind not to speak to you for a whole moon,' she said. 'But when I speak it will hurt you more than if I held my tongue. Therefore listen. This is as true as that the sun is in the sky. Nabata has gone away with Opopa. Not only did I know they were going, but I said to him yesterday when the young moon was in the sky – "Opopa, son of Rejana, listen to me. If you want Nabata for yourself, take her. Do not put off the journey until another moon. Her father will never give her to you. His head is as full of old laws, of old tales and customs of the long-ago, as an ant-hill is full of ants." So they are gone. It would be no use for you to go after them. You can no more catch them than a kangaroo-rat could catch a swan on the wing.'

Erungara stood for a few minutes as if rooted to the earth. Then he said in a broken voice: 'Evil will come to me and mine, for the evil that you have done.' Without another word, he went slowly back to the men's camp.

CHAPTER 2

Next morning Labea found Iliapa still very silent and tearful, and tried to cheer her up by saying that they two would go with nets and a spear, to fish in the Pool of the Laughing Birds. This was a very pretty place two or three miles away, and Iliapa dearly loved to go there. But the thought that she could never do so again with Nabata made her break into a storm of sobs and tears. All her life Nabata had been her constant companion day and night. How could she live without her?

'Now stop crying and come with me,' said Labea with a gentleness that she very rarely showed. 'You know the story of the men who were always stopping to paint themselves with red ochre, so as to be ready for fighting. At last they were turned into the birds that are called Loppa-Loppa, that have breasts as red as flame. If you cry so much something like that may happen to you. How would you like to be turned into a cloud, dropping down rain? You know you are not a little girl now, you are a young woman. Nabata wanted to tell you that she was going away, but I said, "She is too much of a baby. She would cry her eyes out, and then your father would know."'

While Labea was speaking, a boy who was old enough to be in the men's camp, came running up to them and said in breathless haste, 'Some strange young black man wants to see Erungara. But Erungara is lying in his mia-mia, and when I called him he did not answer.'

Labea without a word hurried to the men's camp, followed by Iliapa. The boy ran on ahead, through the thickets of salt-bush that were between the two camps. When they reached Erungara's mia-mia, they found that he was sitting up. As soon as he caught sight of Iliapa, he motioned her to his side. But looking at Labea he held up his hand, palm outward, saying, 'Giver of evil advice, bringer of bad news, trouble me not.'

Labea tossed her head as if about to make a sharp reply. But she checked herself, and went to the back of the mia-mia. Here she was joined by the boy who had brought them the message, and who showed her where the stranger was waiting. It is a strict rule with the Australian natives that a stranger should not come into a camp until he is formally invited to do so. In a few minutes Iliapa was heard calling on her aunt, who at once went round to the front, but kept away from the opening, lest the sight of her should offend the invalid. He was better and wished Ju-ju – the name by which the boy was known – to tell the stranger to come to him. When the young man came, Erungara invited him to sit on a log opposite to himself at the opening of the mia-mia, and tell him his name and why he had come.

'My name is Nalbuka, the son of Apma. . . .'

'Apma of the Plum Tree People,' interrupted Erungara eagerly. 'Your father was the son of Itjina – the cunning hunter. I knew them both well and liked them. If there is anything I can do for you, it is done.'

'Even when I was a small child, I heard my father speak of you as one of the wisest men among the Arunta. A great teacher and a medicine man, who knew how to make the sick well.'

'Have you come that I may make one who is weak strong again?'

'No, that is not what I want,' said Nalbuka. He hesitated and was silent for a little, and then went on: 'I have heard that since the old men of the tribe ill-used you, and cast you from them, you give charms for killing.'

Erungara became very much excited, and gave a long explanation of the matter. He ended by saying: 'My enemies say that I give charms for killing, countrary to the laws for a medicine man and an Oknirabata, for the sake of food. That is a lie. I do but go back to an old long-ago custom, of which they are ignorant. If one comes to me and tells me of a wicked man that has killed some one, who did him no harm, then I give the Lainama, so that the evil one may come to his death.'

'Then you will help me,' said Nalbuka, his eyes flashing with fiery joy. 'My enemy is one who killed a boy, so that he might rob him.'

Erungara covered his face with his hands, and sat for some moments in silence. Ever since his head was so badly hurt, there were times when everything around him seemed to vanish. This feeling came over him now, and he was silent until it passed away.

When it did so, he went to the end of his mia-mia, and brought out a large flat basket, made of two oblong rush mats, sewn together with kangaroo tendon. Out of this basket he took a small parcel that was wrapped in a thick fringe made of emu feathers. Within this there was a curious-looking stone, black in colour, fastened between two sticks bound together with stringy-bark fibre.

'You see one end of this stone is sharpened,' said Erungara. 'That end is for touching men. The other end is blunt and rough; that is for touching women.'

'Touching? not striking?' asked Nalbuka.

'No, no, no, that would bring evil to you and to me,' cried Erungara in a tone of horror. 'You must wait and watch until you find your enemy alone fast asleep. You must then creep up to him, more silently than a snake in the grass. You must not utter a word even below your breath, nor smile for joy that he is in your power. If he is lying on his right side, wait till he turns to the left. Then keep your heart from beating hard when you stoop over him and touch him on the right side.'

Nalbuka, who was listening intently to every word, drew a hard, long breath.

'I can be sure not to utter a word or a sound. I can hold my breath for a time as if I were dead. But how to keep my heart from beating hard – have you got a charm for that? only to think of getting near him makes my heart jump How then can I keep it quiet when I am near enough to touch him?'

'You must train your heart as if it were a little dog,' said the old man sternly. 'Go out at night alone, creep up to a bush and say to yourself, "There is my enemy; I must touch him on the breast, and while I touch him my heart must be as quiet as a little owl fast asleep." Say this and do it, until you teach yourself like men of the long-ago.'

'I will do all as you tell me, and begin this very night alone,' said Nalbuka slowly. Then after a pause: 'How long will it be after I touch him until he is dead?'

'No man can say. It may be after a few sunsets; it may be after many moons. But this I can say to you with a firm tooth – the moment he is hurt after you touch him, he comes to ashes. It may be a fly that stings him in the eye, it may be a puppy that gives him a bite in play, or a 'possum that puts a tooth in him. Once he is touched, the smallest accident will be to him as if a spear were pushed through him in front, and came out at the back.'

Nalbuka drew in his breath, as if already he saw his enemy still in death.

'At last, Ingunta,' he said between his teeth.

'Your head will be in two, if you do not wait for a proper time,' said Erungara angrily. 'You are not ready to try to-morrow even if you had the best chance in the world.'

'Oh no; it is the name that has been given to my enemy. If he was asked to hide in a swamp to snare ducks he would say, Ingunta (To-morrow). If he was asked to hunt kangaroos he would say, Ingunta. If he was asked to look for red and yellow ochre to make ready for a corroboree, he would say, Ingunta. So he came to be called by that name. But one thing he did not put off till to-morrow – to kill a boy when he found him asleep. That was what he did to my young brother who had a silver watch that Ingunta wanted for his own. It was a beautiful watch given to him by a white man he had saved from drowning.'

'Is it long since that took place?' asked Erungara.

'It was after the great rains came – when the creeks boiled and stood up, and carried away trees as if they were reeds and leaves of grass. It was then we left the Big Ranges where I was born.'

Erungara reflected for a moment, and then said, 'That is what the white people would count as nearly a year ago. And your father, where is he now?'

'He was very ill all the way coming from the Big Ranges. Two and two moons after we got to the Roalmah country he died. Then a few weeks after that, my brother was killed. At that time I was riding one day; the horse fell and rolled over me. For more than a moon, I was as one that would never stand up again. When I could walk, Ingunta was far away, and I was too weak to travel more than half a sun in two days. After two moons I was strong. A man of the Wombats said to me, "Ingunta is at Roalmah Station, where there are cows and horses beyond counting." I started for Roalmah. When I was a sun away from the station, one told him that I was on the way. Some men of Jirara had killed a cow. Two police with big guns and little ones were looking for the men of Jirara. Ingunta went to them and he said: "One of the Jirara men that killed the cow is near at hand. His name is Nalbuka: he has the mark of a big cut above the left eye."

'I was walking alone with the moon, and could see the lights of Roalmah far off, when the police came up to me and asked my name. They put bands round my hands, and took me to Looloolo. They put me at night in an iron ilta, with the door shut so that no one could open it, but the police in the day let me lie in the shade of a tree; he gave me to eat and drink more than I wanted.

'One day white men came driving cattle from Roalmah. Gilberka was with them. He is my cousin, and he told me that it was Ingunta who made the police believe that I had helped to kill the cow. He told me that at night in the camp, Ingunta made all the men and boys laugh out loud, turning me into a tale.

'When the sun got up, Gilberka with the white men and the cattle went away. But I lay on the ground. I could not hold up my head. My eyes were shut, but I could not go to sleep.

'After many days and nights a man came from a long way off. He sat in a box in a big room and I stood before him. There was a black man who knew more of the white tongue than I do. He helped me to tell all that I had been doing two suns away from Roalmah when the cow was killed. After the police had spoken, the man in the box said that I was not to be kept any longer in the ilta, or tied by day in the shade of a tree.

'Then I set out for Roalmah. On the way I met Maleka, who is my father's brother. He told me that Ingunta was back at Roalmah, and that part of his work is to take food in a cart to the white men who look after sheep and cattle a sun or more away from the big house of the station. Maleka was going one way and I was going another. But he turned and came some of the way with me and this is what he said: "You are right to take the life of the man who killed your young brother, so as to get his watch. But if you kill him with your hands, the white men will surely find you. You may go to the east or you may go to the west, you may hide by the far-away swamps, or go to the great salt water that has but one shore. But they will find you. Not because they are so cunning, but because they can get a black tracker to help them. Go to Erungara, he will know how to help you. So I came to you."'

'You have done well,' said Erungara, 'to take your uncle's advice.' He wrapped a piece of the emu fringe round the stone and gave it to Nalbuka, saying: 'Let no one look upon it, and when you have touched Ingunta with it, bring it back to me in the same state that I give it to you. Do not forget a word that I have said to you.'

'I will not forget one word that you have spoken,' said Nalbuka. He went away walking so fast, that in two or three minutes he was lost to sight among the trees.

CHAPTER 3

It was nearly three weeks after his first visit, when Nalbuka came again to Erungara, a couple of hours before the sun went down.

'Have you brought me back the Lainama?' asked the old man.

'Yes, I have it here.' Nalbuka's voice was low, and his breathing was hurried like that of one who has been running. As he spoke, he pointed to the rush basket that he carried with his spear, his boomerang and his shield. Erungara motioned him to sit down, and he did so.

'I have brought you an aroa that I killed on the way; he is not fat, but he is young,' he said, taking a rock-wallaby out of his basket as he spoke. All the time Erungara was gazing at him steadily. Nalbuka knew this, and did not once look into the old man's eyes.

'This is the Lainama,' he said, handing the stone back, wrapped in the fringe of emu feathers, and tied round with a piece of bark fibre, just as it was given to him.

'Did you keep in mind all that I told you?' As the old man spoke there was a look of fear in his face.

There was a pause before Nalbuka made reply, and when he did so, his voice was not quite even as he said, 'I have brought it back safe and no eyes have looked at it but my own.'

Erungara untied the string, and unfolded the fringe of emu feathers. The moment that his eyes fell on the strange black stone, sharp at one end and rough at the other, he gave a cry of horror.

'Alua, Alua, Alua,' he wailed. This is the Arunta word for blood, and as he said it, his voice, though not loud, was so full of terror, that Iliapa, who, with two other girls, sat a little way off making bracelets from topknot feathers of the sulphur-crested cockatoos, came running up in fear that some evil had come to her father.

'Go back, go back, I did not call you,' he cried, hiding the stone so that she should not see it. When she had gone, he turned to Nalbuka and said to him sternly, 'You said that you had brought the Lainama back safe, but what is this dark stain?'

'It is the blood of my enemy,' said Nalbuka, with the voice as of one in a dream.

'Did I not warn you?' said Erungara, now more in sorrow than in anger. 'Do you know the danger that you have cast round yourself and around me by going against the old laws and customs of our people?'

'Things did not come about in the way you think,' said Nalbuka, speaking slowly, like one who finds it hard to get at the words he wants to use. He leant his face on his hands, and was silent for some minutes. Then looking up, he said, 'I will tell you all, as things came to pass without any changing or twisting. Night after night I went out by the creek alone, and taught my heart to keep still. I stood by a salt-bush at a bend of the Tekua, where the sun has drunk up all the water, and I said to myself, "There is Ingunta. He is lying fast asleep on the left side. Touch him on the breast, with your heart as still as a little brown owl asleep at mid-day. Then creep away as if you were a snake in the grass. . . . "'

'You kept well in mind all that I taught you, and yet there has been a shedding of blood,' whispered Erungara, who kept looking at the dull mark on the stone as if he could not turn his eyes away from the sight.

'The shedding of blood did not take place in the way you think. But let me tell you all things as they came. When my heart no longer jumped or went fast at the thought of Ingunta nearer to me than my shadow, I went to Maleka, my father's brother. He was sitting down half a sun from the Big House of Roalmah. Maleka is still strong, but his wife is weak and blind, one son is dead, the other has gone lost. Sometimes hunger is upon him, for his wife cries if he leaves her. I snared three ducks at the Unkwala Swamp, and brought them to him. He was glad and said, "What I can do for you I will do, for you are to me as a son."'

'"Do this," I said to him. "Go to the house of Roalmah, and find out where Ingunta will be for one, two and three suns. This is not for killing; it is to touch him with the Lainama, and I must know where to get him when he is asleep."'

'Maleka went away next day when the stars were still in the sky, and he came back when the sun was gone. The widow of the son who is dead works at the Big House, and she told him all that I wished to know. In two days Ingunta was going with rations to the boundary-rider who is at the Wonka Creek, and when he went there he stayed all night. On the morning of the day he was to go, I went off before the east was red, and got close to the Wonka before the stars came out. When the light was gone, I walked in the scrub by the creek till the boundary-rider's hut was in sight. He was sitting at the door, and his two sheep-dogs were tied up where some sheep were camped, so that if any dingoes came they would bark and let him know.

'While I was watching, Ingunta drove up in the spring-cart. The boundary-rider gave a cry of gladness, as he got hold of a jar, and poured drink out of it into a pannikin. I knew it was strong drink that Ingunta had got at the little public-house near the Swamp of the Curlews. My mind grew easy. They would both drink till deep sleep fell on them. I went by the Wonka till I came to a small water hole. Here I ate and drank and smoked, till sleep came on me. When I woke I knew by the stars it was some time after midnight.

'I went quickly to the boundary-rider's hut. Before it came in sight I heard angry shouting, two talking at the same time. Then I heard Ingunta calling out a very bad name. There came a sound as of something smashing on the ground. After that all was quiet. Not one more word was spoken. It would be strange if two men in fierce anger fell asleep so soon.

'I waited for a long time. The dogs barked hard, but no sound came from the hut. I went softly close up to it. Ingunta was under a mulga – lying on his left side. I would not have to wait for him to turn over. I went close up and bent over him. All things turned round, and the Lainama fell from my hand. I took it up and it was red. The blood had poured from his head to his right breast. . . .'

'The blood had poured from his head . . .' gasped Erungara slowly.

'Yes, from a great wound made by the big thick bottle lying at his head in pieces. That was the sound I heard when all got still. The boundary-man had killed him. I crept up to him mad with hate. Now I was cold. I wanted to lie down and cry. I heard a noise. The white man had come out of the hut, with crooked steps, going from side to side. He said to me, "Here – you nigger – what have you done to Ingunta? I must go and tell the police." Hearing the dogs bark, he stumbled and fell over saying, "You are a wicked nigger to do such a thing – the sight has made me so bad, I must go to sleep." That night I got to Maleka and told him all as I have told you now. He wept like a child, fearing that the lies of the white man may put me in danger.'

'Many times the evil that the white man does is put upon the black man,' said Erungara.

When he found that Nalbuka had not used the Lainama in a wrong way, a great fear was lifted from his mind. When he saw the young man with the look of one who is in heavy trouble, silent and downcast, he tried to lighten his gloom by talk of other days.

'Before the white men came we were a great people. The old men were held in honour; they took care of the holy things, and trained the boys to be young men, and taught them the laws of the Arunta. They taught them how to bear pain and hunger, and how to cast fear from them; they taught them how to kill the birds of the air and of the water, how to snare the great beasts and the small; what things might be eaten, and what should not be touched. They taught them the days of corroboree and dance, and the days of going without food. They taught them of their relations on the side of the father and the mother, telling them what women they may marry, and what women they must not look at. Now the young are as crows that pick up a bone and a mate as it pleases them. But you, Nalbuka, are not as these. When I saw the stain of blood, and thought you had not taken heed to my words, great fear fell upon me. You have obeyed – yet your enemy is dead; it is well.'

Nalbuka sat with his head bent like a rush in a storm. He looked up and said:

'Yes, the man who killed my brother when he was a boy and asleep, will walk about no more. But that gives me no joy. Not long ago they tied me up for killing a cow I never saw. What tale will the white man tell of the black man he found beside Ingunta? To my face he . . . '

'Did you hear the news that has come from Roalmah?' cried Aunt Labea, coming as quickly before her brother's mia-mia as if she had sprung from the ground. Without waiting for a reply she went on, her words coming so fast that she hardly took time to draw her breath: 'Rankaraka and his boy have just come in from fishing, they met one from Roalmah who told them all. Lantara who is called Ingunta has been killed at the hut of the boundary-man by the Wonka. When he brought the news to Roalmah, he was crying like a child that sucks at his mother's breast. He says he was sleeping, and when he woke up he found Ingunta dead with a black man standing beside him.'

Nalbuka turned to the old man with a meaning look. But Erungara, who knew that Labea had very sharp sight, did not return the glance, merely saying in a careless way: 'Most of what you are saying may be a tale as idle as the screaming of grass-parrots.'

Labea was so angry at having her news treated so coldly that she went away at once with a scornful laugh. When she got a few paces away, she turned, saying, 'If I told you old lies about fish walking on their tails in the trees, and of stars turning into babies, you would believe every word.'

'There is no one that can make a tale out of a look faster than Labea,' said the old man as soon as his sister was out of hearing. 'You are spent with walking much and eating little; when she told of the boundary-man's lie, your face became as that of one who is found out, so I made her angry that she might not look at you. As you taught your heart to be still, so you must keep your face as one who knows nothing, if you hear them talk of the man who is dead.'

'I may keep my face as one who knows nothing,' replied Nalbuka in a low voice, 'but who can tell what a new day may bring? I waited and longed with all my heart to touch my enemy for death, yet when I found him dead, it is as if I could weep for wishing him harm.'

This was a feeling beyond the old medicine man and conjurer. He had given the Lainama so that it might cause Ingunta's death. But when he thought the stone had been used contrary to the old laws, he turned faint with terror, not because of the guilt of shedding blood, but the fear of breaking a ritual. But this had not been done and he had no sense of wrong in planning a death according to the old custom. He could almost have laughed at Nalbuka's horror on finding his enemy slain. He had the tribal feeling of right and wrong; but an emotion moved the young man akin to the individual conscience. But Erungara in his own way was a kindly old man, and instead of showing that Nalbuka's lack of reason amused him, he said in a soothing voice: 'Now it is time you ate and drank. Then if the grip of sleep does not come on you, we can think where you should stay till the talk of what took place at Wonka Creek dies away.'

CHAPTER 4

Erungara and Nalbuka talked late into the night. Though they had known each other for so short a time, the secrets they shared made them feel like old friends.

Many of the blacks are great at yarning. If you are near one of their camps at night you may sometimes hear them talking away as if they did not mean to sleep till dawn. Erungara had got into this way of much speaking when there was any one to listen to him. But after a time Nalbuka's eyes began to close. He had slept very little for some nights, and in less than two days he had walked more than fifty miles. And all the time he was carrying a spear, a shield, a waddy, a boomerang, and the netted bag, that amongst other things held the Lainama and some food.

'You are worn out and no wonder,' said Erungara. 'Lie down and sleep well; then in the morning I will tell you what I think you had better do. Put this under your head.' As he spoke Erungara handed the young man an opossum rug. Nalbuka lay down outside the mia-mia with the rug under his head and was soon fast asleep.

Erungara lay awake for some time thinking over many things. 'That will be best; he will be safer there,' he said at last half-aloud. Then he, too, fell asleep. But when dawn was creeping into the east, he was awakened all at once by one talking in a loud angry voice:

'It is true, it is true. The thing I longed for with all my bowels was to see Ingunta dead. It was mirth to me at night alone and food in the morning, when I thought of the hour when he would be cold and stiff and never more see the light of the sun. It is true that I crept up to him when he lay on his side to touch him for death. But what did I find? He was lying in his blood, killed by the boundary-man to whom he brought strong drink. Even to my face the man threw his own act upon me. Now you come to tie my hands and to lock me up, as you did for killing a cow I never saw. But no, no, you will never take me alive. Before you lay a finger on me I will kill you where you stand.'

As he spoke Nalbuka sprang to the side of the mia-mia and caught up his spear and his shield.

'Nalbuka, Nalbuka, you are in a dream; wake up and see. I am not an enemy, I am your friend,' said Erungara in a firm gentle voice. But Nalbuka was not asleep. His eyes were wide open and he stared hard at the old man as if trying to make out who he was. Erungara stood by his side and passed his right hand a few times across his forehead.

Nalbuka drew a long breath and looked carefully all round.

'Where are they? Have the police gone away?' he said, speaking more slowly, in a half-dazed voice.

'There are no police – no one at all to harm you. Sit down and I will give you some of the tobacco they sent me from Balkara.' While Erungara was speaking he took the spear and shield out of Nalbuka's hands, placed the 'possum rug for him at the front of the mia-mia, gave him a stick of tobacco and then went to kindle the fire and put a quart pot of water on it to make some tea.

When he made this he brought a pannikin full of it and a piece of Johnny-cake to Nalbuka. He himself seldom ate till mid-day, but he got his pipe and lit it and sat within the mia-mia and pressed the young man to eat and drink. But though Nalbuka drank the tea, he had no wish for food.

'You say there is no one to do me harm,' he said after sitting in silence for some moments.

'But well do I know that the policeman who tied my hands and locked me up for killing the cow I never saw, was sorry when I was let go. He will hear the boundary-man's story. One here and there will say, "Yes, Ingunta killed Nalbuka's young brother." "Where was Nalbuka when the killing took place?" the policeman will say. Then bit by bit my life will be thrown to the dogs. Even you yourself, Erungara, could hardly tell the truth from the lie. The Lainama you gave me was stained with his blood; I did stand over him while his body was yet warm. In my dream I saw it all as clear as you see a lake under the sun. Before I fell asleep I said to myself, "If there is trouble I will flee away over the desert till I come to the Great Salt Water." Then a voice inside me said, "No, stay where you are; if they come after you – fight." That was what I did when I saw them coming to tie my hands and lock me up. Yes, saw them, though I stood on my feet and my eyes were open, as you know. Well, I will not hide, I will not run away over hills of sand, hot as flame to the skin, where not a leaf grows, nor a lizard crawls. I am all alone. My father is dead; my brother is killed; I have no mother to care for me, no woman to give me joy. All the time sorrow would be nearer to me than my shadow; hunger and thirst and fear would be with me day and night.'

'Your words make me glad,' said Erungara, 'for there are more reasons than you know why you should not run away because of what took place at Wonka Creek. You are right to think that the policeman who has been in the Roalmah District for many years was sorry when you were set free. It has always been his way to believe evil of the black man, even though he should do as little harm as the child who sucks. But a few days ago this police trooper had a bad fall from his horse. He has been taken away to be put in a house for the sick, and may never come back, and there is a new man in his place. And more than that, I want you to come with me to Balkara.'

'To Balkara? The big station where they have such fine horses.'

'Yes, fine horses and fine sheep and cattle,' said Erungara, 'and where the Master is one of the best friends the blacks ever had in this country. A long time ago, I was camping in a thick scrub nearly a day's walking from the Big House of the station. One night I heard voices, then low crying. I rose and went near the camp of the women, where my two girls were, and called out, "Is one of you crying?" Their aunt told me they were both asleep. But a little voice in the scrub beyond cried out, "Coo-ee, Coo-ee." It was a little boy and girl of Balkara who had strayed away from their home and been lost for two days. The woman-child was the youngest, and was so weak she could hardly walk.

'The next day when they were rested and made strong with food, I took them back to the Big House. When the woman-child was tired I carried her. They made me stay a night, then they took me in a buggy to the camp and got my two girls to come back with me to Balkara, where we stayed till I had to go to a distance to meet some of the tribe who were still friendly to me. When we were leaving, the Master and the Missus said to us: "If you are in any trouble, if one of you is ill, if there is anything we can do for you at any time, come to us. It will make us glad to have you here at any time." Three days ago a white man came here from Balkara, with a pack-horse, bringing flour and sugar and tea and jam and fruit in bottles, with many other things of which I know not the name, but are good to eat. They heard that I was alone and ill and that I was able to walk but little. You know how in a tale that goes from one to the other a butterfly grows into an emu.

'Besides these things the white man brought me a message. The people of Balkara wish me to go there and stay with them always. Also he asked me if I knew of any young black man who could ride and would be good at station work. I told him I would ask my sister's sons who work at Roalmah, if they knew of one. I have not done so yet. Last night it came into my head that it would be the best place for you. What do you say?'

Nalbuka, who was listening with great care to all that Erungara said, did not reply at once. He put down the pipe he had been smoking, and stood up and stretched himself, looking across the woods to the east where the sun was now shining large and red almost with the splendour of a summer morning. Then, facing Erungara, he said:

'I can ride, muster cattle, and look after sheep; I can help to dig wells and clean out tanks, and put up fences. But after a time I am tired of the white man and his ways, saying always to-day what must be done to-morrow, or when the next moon comes. When I get tired I want to go Bush – to hunt and fish and snare birds, to lie down when I want to, and get up when I wash. If . . .'

'Come then and find for yourself how good the Master of Balkara is, and how he thinks of these things, and will let you go Bush when you get tired and come back when you are hungry,' said Erungara with eager haste. 'But there may be some other place you want to go to, where you have friends that you like,' he added more slowly, half in doubt, half by way of asking a question.

'My father's brother, Maleka, would be glad if I was with him. But his wife is blind and weak and would not leave Roalmah, where they are good to her, when they do not forget that she is alive. It would be very foolish for me, as you know, to sit down in that place. Yes, I will come with you to Balkara. It may be long before my feet ache to wander again. I am tired of being alone.'

'Then we will start to-morrow,' said Erungara in a voice full of content. 'It is a journey of two suns. Let us rest before we begin to get ready. Our night was cut short by dreams, that daylight has eaten up like a cloud without rain.'

'Yet on a day when we do not look for it the cloud may come back full of storm and lightning,' replied Nalbuka in a brooding tone. Sorrow and care had been with him so long – he could not all at once shake off the gloom that had settled on him.

He lay down at the far end of the mia-mia, Erungara at the opening. In a short time both were fast asleep.

CHAPTER 5

When Erungara woke up, the first one he saw was his sister Labea, who was sitting not far from his mia-mia under the meagre shade of a stringy bark sapling working at a handsome fringe of emu feathers, on which she had been engaged from time to time, for many months.

'You have had a long sleep,' she said, 'and I have been waiting here since the sun got high, to tell you something you ought to know.'

'What about?' asked Erungara quickly, instantly thinking of some new danger for Nalbuka.

'I was down fishing in the creek this morning early,' replied Labea, 'when who should pass by but Wirno, from Roalmah, looking for a horse that is lost. "Have you heard about Yukuta?" said he to me. "He is going to the cattle station the Roalmah people have near the Big Salt Water and he does not now want the child of your brother for his wife." "That is a lucky thing for the child of my brother," said I. "Iliapa is a fine young girl, and ought to have a strong man to hunt for her, to fight for her, not a man as old as her father, and with the ways of an evil snake."'

'So that is the news you have for me?' said Erungara, looking hard at his sister, wondering whether it was all true, or whether it was partly a made-up story. For he knew that if Labea had an object in doing so, she could make a few words into a long tale.

'Yes, that is the news I have for you, make what you like of it,' said Labea calmly. 'Now I must go and get on as fast as I can with this fringe. The Mistress of Roalmah wants it before another moon is over. She will be so proud of it. She can hang it above a window, or round her bed or above the fireplace. She will give me meat, bread and tobacco as long as I live.'

As she was going away, Labea cast a searching glance beyond her brother into the mia-mia where Nalbuka lay still fast asleep; a picture of youthful strength, as great a contrast to the old man of whom Labea had been speaking as could be well seen.

When she got to her own mia-mia, she found Iliapa busy turning out one of those big netted bags in which aboriginal women and girls keep the odds and ends they value most. At the bottom she had found a broken comb, a brush, and a piece of red ribbon, almost quite new. These belonged to the time when Iliapa had stayed with her father and sister at Balkara. If there was a place in the world that Iliapa loved, it was this same Balkara. Ever since the white man had come with the message and gifts to her father, she hoped day and night that he would go back there. The Mistress there had been so good to herself and Nabata, taught them how to sew, how to count at card games, and play with the children, and keep themselves quite neat and tidy. Thinking of this, Iliapa began to brush out her hair. She had for some time past used only a native wooden comb, so that her hair had got tangled in places. Now she brushed hard at it until it was quite smooth; then she plaited it in the way that Missus taught her, and fastened up the plait at the end by tying the piece of bright red ribbon round it.

Aunt Labea, who had filled a black clay pipe with tobacco, was now slowly smoking as she went on working at the emu fringe, and watching Iliapa from time to time with the keen bright eye that was left to her. In her young days she had been restless as the waves, save when she slept. She was, however, quiet enough now, and would sometimes pass whole days smoking, and working at some native craft. Then, as if suddenly waking up, tell tales of the long-ago – of the strange things that happened in those days to men and women, to children and birds, and the beasts of the wood. When doing so, she would sometimes laugh and talk in a loud shrill way that could be heard far off from her mia-mia.

As she watched Iliapa tying up her plaited hair with the piece of red ribbon, she took the pipe out of her mouth and laughed.

'Labea, why are you laughing?' asked Iliapa, with some surprise.

'I am laughing at the look of the red string in your black hair,' replied Labea. 'Perhaps you are expecting to see Yukuta soon, and that is why you are making yourself so fine.'

'Ah, don't speak of him, don't speak of him. You know very well I hate the thought of him,' said the girl, with the tears rising in her eyes.

'What would you give me if I made up a plan so that you would never have to see him?' asked Labea. Iliapa looked at her aunt for a little in silence.

'What would I give you?' she repeated. 'Anything that I have in the world. Do you care for this, or this, or this?' she cried, holding up one after the other, a plume of hawk's feathers, another of the sulphur-coloured crests of white cockatoos, then bracelets of the red seeds of plants.

'Would you give me your baby 'possum?'

The baby 'possum was at that moment fast asleep under a corner of Iliapa's Balkara blanket, all curled up with his tail round his nose.

'You would not really like my little Popo,' said Iliapa. 'He runs about so much at night; he would jump on you, and pull your hair. You see, I don't mind, because I can go to sleep the next minute, but he would make you fearfully cross.'

Aunt Labea laughed louder than before. 'You have some of the cunning of the old medicine man in you,' she said. 'But never mind, the plan has been made. Only you must play your part. You must not keep on being as quiet as Popo is when the sun is shining. When I was fishing in the creek early this morning, I saw one from Roalmah, and heard some news of Yukuta. I sat by your father's mia-mia until he woke up. As soon as he opened his eyes I said to him, "Yukuta is going far away – he no longer wants your daughter to be his wife."'

'Oh, Labea, I am so glad,' cried Iliapa, clapping her hands for joy. 'What did father say, what did father say?'

'Your father is one who often says a good deal by not speaking,' said Labea. 'He looked at me long as if trying to see my very inside. But I kept my face, and said with a firm tooth, "That is the news I have for you," and I came away. Now do you know what you must do?'

'Tell me, tell me. I will do it at once; even if I am afraid, still I will do it,' said Iliapa eagerly.

'Pooh! what should you be afriad of? A girl is not as strong as a man; but when he knows how to do a thing in three ways, she knows how to do it three and three times. Go to your father, running and laughing, and cry out before you reach him, "Oh, father, I am so glad Yukuta has gone far away, and he will never come for me. Now I can be happy like Nabata, without running away from you as she did."'

'Must I say it just like that?' asked Iliapa, who had never spoken to her father of Nabata's flight, and feared that to do so might make him angry.

'Yes, you must say it word for word, just like that. Say it over after me, so that you will not forget a word, or put it in the wrong place.'

Iliapa obeyed, and when she had said, without a mistake, the little speech her aunt made for her, she set out on her errand. But when she had got a few paces away, Labea called her back.

'There is one thing I want to ask you,' she said. 'Do you know that the young man who came the day after Nabata went away is in your father's mia-mia?'

'No, I did not know – my father did not tell me.'

'Well, tell me over again what you are going to say.'

Iliapa did so, word perfect, and then was allowed to go.

She was not away very long, and when she came back, her eyes were shining with pleasure.

'Labea, we are going away to-morrow at sunrise. We are going to Balkara,' she said, her voice trembling with excitement.

'But why don't you tell your story from the beginning, and not jump into the middle, like a 'possum that has been hit on the head, and falls from a gum-tree?' said Aunt Labea crossly.

'This news about going to Balkara has put other things from me – it makes me so glad – I only want to think about that and getting ready. It is stupid of me but I cannot help it,' said Iliapa meekly. 'Yes – I think I said what you told me all right – even that about being happy like Nabata, without running away. When he heard it, father looked at me a long time and said, "Who put that into your mouth about running away? It belongs to an old head, not to yours."'

'The old wombat – he meant me,' said Labea with some anger. 'But I have spoilt some of his plans of sticking to the rules and the tales of the long-ago. I sent Yukuta a message in his name after Nabata went away. So now your father is going to Balkara, and you are going away to-morrow. Do you know if the young man is going there?'

'Yes, he is. Father had cooked a rock-wallaby – I think the young man brought it last night. They were eating it and busy talking when I got there. The young man's name is Nalbuka. Father used to know his people long ago. He must have come now from far away. Father said to him, "Rest to-day, and to-morrow we leave at daylight." Now is it not a good thing I took care of that last dress Missus gave me; it is quite good for me to wear when we go to Balkara.'

While Iliapa was speaking, she had turned out a bundle of her things that were at the back of the mia-mia. Among them was a skirt and blouse of strong dark blue Galatea. There was a rent under one of the arms, and Iliapa had a great search for a needle and a reel of cotton with which to mend this. The thimble that had been given to her she lost one day down by the creek, when she and Nabata had been amusing themselves by sewing leaves together for little wooden dolls. When Aunt Labea saw her threading a needle and beginning to sew up the rent in her blouse, she began to laugh as if it were a great joke. She herself had sewn the skins of animals together hundreds of times by means of a bone piercer, made quite sharp at one end, using for thread kangaroo tendon or strong bark fibre. But to sew with a tiny sharp steel thing, with a thread so thin that it could hardly be seen, seemed to her a comic sight.

For all that, when Iliapa had done her mending, Aunt Labea helped her to decide which were the things that she must take with her. These were the chief articles:

1 cloak made of wild-cat skin.
1 small blue blanket.
1 stick for digging yelka – a kind of yam – the other end formed to help in climbing trees.
1 net for catching fish in creeks and swamps.
1 pitchi – a small trough, hollowed out of a piece of beanwood, used for carrying water or food.
2 semi-cylindrical pieces of the flower stalk of a grass-tree, used for kindling fire by rubbing.

The netted bag, for odds and ends.

As for things like the small shield, with figures of birds carved on it, and skin rolled and prepared on which to beat time at corroborees, round and flat baskets, etc., it was impossible to take them all.

'I can keep them for you,' said Labea. 'You will be coming back one day.' So they made a heap of the articles to be left, and then Iliapa went on folding and tying together those that she would take with her. While she was at work, she kept crooning the words of a song:

Miny-el-ity yarluke an-ambe
Aly-el-arr yerk-in yangaiak-ar

until her aunt said, in a sharp way, 'What is that you are singing? It sounds as if you were cursing in a strange tongue.'

'There is not a word of cursing in it,' said Iliapa, laughing. 'It means walking among fine hills, with trees and grass. It is part of the song of the Adelaide natives. Polde taught it to me when I was at Balkara. She came from far away with a white woman and her family, who live a sun away from Balkara. But Polde did not like staying with white people all the time – she was in the camp near Balkara when we were there.'

'It is not lucky to sing a song in a strange tongue,' said Labea, cutting up some tobacco to fill her pipe afresh.

Iliapa, who felt so happy that she could not do a thing or utter a word to cause the least trouble to anyone, instantly stopped crooning the Adelaide song, and sang instead some words she had often heard her aunt chanting.

CHAPTER 6

When Iliapa left her father to hurry back and get ready for the journey on which they were to set out, early next morning, he sat for some time without saying a word. Then he roused himself, and turning to Nalbuka, he said, 'You see how it is with me now. It is good I have a place to go to in my old age. Once I was a great man among our people, but now I am as one of no account. Yukuta, to whom I promised my girl, because of keeping to the old laws, sends word to break the bargain with as little care as he would spill water when the rain was falling.'

'I have heard evil things of this Yukuta; he is old and cruel. To me, it seems a good thing, that he does not come for your daughter. She would hate him, and he would be wicked to her,' said Nalbuka, with a directness that was part of his character.

Erungara looked at him with a startled air, as if a new thought had all at once come into his head. Before he could frame a reply, the young man spoke again.

'My mother died at the time of the greatest of all rains, when the creeks spread into bogs, and the lakes and swamps were like the Great Salt Water. My father, as I told you, died when the white people took me for killing a cow I never saw. You know about my young brother. Once I was never far from some of my own people. Now I am alone all the time. Give your daughter to me for my wife when she is a little older, and I will be to you as a son.'

The old man sat for some time without making any reply. Then he spoke: 'Your words are good. After we get to Balkara, at the time when the young turkeys leave their nest next season, I will give you Iliapa.'

'I am glad,' said Nalbuka in a low voice. 'When Iliapa came to you with joy in her face, because the old man to whom she was promised was going far off, I said to myself, "This daughter of Erungara is good, and good to look at. What if he would give her to me?" Now it is even so. You have given your word, and all is well with me.'

They talked for some little time longer, finding comfort in the friendship that they had one for the other. When they slept, no evil dreams came to them, and they rose up to set out for Balkara, while the light was still so faint, that you could hardly tell a white thread from a black one. But early as it was, Iliapa was up before them. She had her bundle all ready, and Labea was grumbling at being awakened as she said in the middle of the night. But when she saw Nalbuka swinging Iliapa's bundle over his shoulders, along with her father's baskets, leaving the girl only Popo, and her netted bag to carry, then a smile of triumph lighted up the haggard old face.

She went a little part of the way with the travellers, first walking beside her brother, while Nalbuka stalked on ahead, and Iliapa brought up the rear.

'I am glad you have found a son in yur old age,' said Labea, 'who is strong and young, and a cunning hunter. After he has been your son for a little time, will he then be your son-in-law? Or am I only making up a dream in the way I like it?'

'This much I will tell you,' replied Erungara. 'There is no need for you to help Iliapa to run away so that she may have a young man for her husband.'

Aunt Labea gave one of her shrill laughs, and then dropped behind to speak to Iliapa.

'You have often called me a very cross old woman, and told me I lost my eye because of my bad temper,' she said.

'But that was when you made me into ugly rhymes and stories,' said Iliapa, now feeling sorry that she had sometimes said such things when Aunt Labea made her angry.

'So it might be. But when you are proud that you have a tall, fine, strong young man for yourself, just think this. It was old Labea, with the one eye and the bad temper and the white hair, who sent a mocking message to Yukuta, that made him send an answer back to your father, "I no longer want your girl." Now I must turn back, today I finish the handsome emu fringe. After this I get bread and meat and tobacco from the Mistress of Roalmah, as long as I live. My sons can hunt for me or not, as they like.'

So there, at a turn of the road, where a low range came into sight in the red light of the dawn, the old woman said good-bye. To Nalbuka, she said something in a low voice, which neither father nor daughter heard. It must have been some joke, for it made the young man laugh out loud. When she had got a few paces on her way back, she began to chant a song that she made up as she went; her thin, shrill voice, with a curious crack in it, now and then, as if it broke in two:–

'Who are the three that I see going away before the sun shows his face? They are the father and his child, and a son-in-law. And what sort of a son-in-law? Is it an old man with a bent back, with white hair and the marks upon his face of many fights, with the wicked eyes of one that has the temper of an evil snake? No, no, no, this is a young man, tall, and straight and strong. Who are the three that I see?' etc., etc.

It was on the morning of the third day after leaving the Jimarra, that the travellers saw the smoke of native fires near the Balkara half a mile from the Big House. A few minutes after they saw the smoke, a young black woman who was fishing at a large pool of the river caught sight of them and came running towards them, calling out at the pitch of her voice, 'Iliapa, Iliapa.'

No sooner did Iliapa see and hear her than she also ran to meet her, calling out, 'Polde, Polde,' in a voice of joy. They hugged each other, held each other's hands, laughed and talked so fast all at the same moment, that neither heard what the other said. Then Polde burst into tears, even sobbing a little.

'But, Polde, why do you cry?' said Iliapa, with a little dismay.

'Don't you know I always cry when I am very glad?' said Polde, smiling through her tears. 'Oh, I am so happy you have come, there is no other girl I care for so much. I have caught some nice little fish that I will cook for your breakfast. But first I will run and tell the Missus you have come.'

Polde ran as fast as her feet could carry her straight to the Big House, where Missus sat on the veranda reading. She was near the open window of the schoolroom, where the two children who had been lost, for a day and a half and two nights, more than a year ago, were now at lessons with their governess.

The mother could never forget the fear and misery of that time. They had been let out of school a little after one o'clock, and when luncheon, which was the children's dinner, was over, they had played for a time at being bushrangers, in the sitting-room, until their mother, who was lying down on the sofa, asked them to go into the veranda, where they could make as much noise as they liked, without tiring anyone. Then she had fallen asleep, and when she woke up, the governess had brought her in a cup of tea, saying, 'I thought the children were here.'

'So they were, until I asked them to go and play in the veranda. Perhaps you had better call them in for some tea. Helen did not eat much dinner.'

The governess went to call the children, but they were nowhere to be found.

There was no alarm for some time, but in a few hours every one on the place was searching far and near. The worst of it was, that some black men who would have been skilful in tracking them, were absent at a corroboree, and the father had gone on some business to a neighbouring station thirty-five miles away. When he came back on the following day, he found every one searching for the children, while their poor mother, almost out of her mind with fear, could do nothing but walk up and down by the Balkara, where there were big water-holes that never dried up, even in the hottest summers. This had always been a favourite place with the children, for there was fish in the water – it was here Polde was catching some on this morning – and always many water-birds coming and going. The mother could not get it out of her head that the children had gone to this part of the creek, and fallen in, one perhaps in trying to save the other.

In this terrible suspense nearly two days and two full nights went by, all the station people scouring the country in every likely and unlikely place. The mother, more dead than alive with fatigue and misery, was lying helpless, on the afternoon of the second day, when all at once she heard the governess crying out in a glad voice, 'The children, the children!'

Oh what a sight of joy it was to see them alive and well, with that good old Erungara, who had fed and cared for them and brought them back in safety!

Now when Polde came flying with the news of his arrival, the children claimed a half-holiday, to go with their mother to see him. Also Iliapa and the strange young man that Polde said looked as if he belonged to Erungara. The governess, nothing loath, fell in with the plan. So the new arrivals had a great welcome and a bountiful breakfast, which, strange to say, the Chinese cook got ready without a single grumble at the extra trouble. For Ching Meng was very fond of the children and remembered very well how Erungara had brought them back safe and sound when the whole station was in despair, thinking they would never see them again alive.

A week after his arrival, the Mistress of Balkara came to speak to Erungara about Iliapa.

'She is so steady and useful,' she said, 'I want her to come for a part of each day to me at the house, and learn to do things. She is not like Polde, who is so very quick, and can pick up anything in a short time, but cannot bear any regular work for more than a few days. Iliapa does not learn so quickly, but then she does not get tired, and want to go away. She is happy to go on doing things day after day, and she does not forget.'

Erungara liked to hear his daughter praised, and he listened to all that Missus had to say with a pleased look. Then he said slowly in his broken English, that as long as Iliapa belonged to him, she could go every day to the Big House, and learn whatever Missus wished to teach her. But he had promised her to Nalbuka, and she would be his wife when the young turkeys learned to fly next season. After that she must obey Nalbuka, even if he asked her to go away with him to the Big Ranges. Missus was greatly interested in this piece of news. Nalbuka had been found very useful for station work, especially among horses. 'I can trust him in the stable better than anyone on the place,' the Master said of him in a short time after he came to the station.

'I am glad you will have such a good son in your old age,' said Missus. 'When Nalbuka gets tired of work, the Master will let him take a holiday in the Bush. He and Iliapa can always have a home here. As for you, Erungara, you will not want to go wandering about any more. Well, in the meantime, Iliapa can come to me every day. Perhaps she will get Polde to come with her.'

But Polde's views on this matter were of the clearest.

'When I was a pickaninny,' she said, 'my people sat down for a long time at Moorano. The children of Moorano were good to me, and gave me red dresses and ribbons and shoes and lollies, and often so much cake, that I must lie down in the shade and roll about till my inside got better. They had cupboards and cupboards with books full of pictures. The biggest girl showed me how to read some of the little books, with kangaroos that talked and emus that made bread, and dogs and cats that stood on their hind legs, in hats and clothes. When the mother of the children heard me read she was pleased and said I should come into the schoolroom every day and learn more. Sit down and put my nose in a copy-book and make black marks, and spell long words without looking in the book. To do that every day was more stupid than to be a wombat in a hole in the dirt. Yes, the mother of these good children of Moorano, she want me to sit down, and do the same thing all over, one day and the next and the day after, for ever and ever. It made me bad outside and inside, and all over me. One day I want to eat my tucker, and do nothing but lie in the shade. No, I never sit down all the days with white people. They are some of them good, but every one of them a small bit cranky. When they done one thing, they run to do the next, and before that is done they run off to do more. Some days I will come with you, but some days I want to run about, or be like your Popo, who gets into a corner with his face tucked away in his fur.'

CHAPTER 7

At the time when the young turkeys were learning to fly, Iliapa became the wife of Nalbuka, the summer after they went to Balkara. In less than a year, a fine boy was born to them, whom they called Alibaka. He was barely a year old when he began to walk, and when he was a year and a half, his mouth was full of little teeth as white as pearls, which were often in full view as he smiled, and laughed and crowed, and lisped out words from morning till night. It would be hard to say which of the three was proudest of him – his father, his mother, or his grandfather. But no one else in the world could love him quite as much as his mother did.

When the little fellow was between four and five years of age, it was curious to see how constantly he was with his grandfather. Erungara had by this time got rather deaf, but his sight was almost as keen as ever. He had no aches or pain, and his old age was made happy by the company of this bright little child, full of life, and fun, and wonder at all that he saw, from the birds flying in the air, to the strange things that were in the old man's big flat basket. Alibaka would turn over, and pull out one object after the other, that no one else had ever dared to look at, much less touch.

'I do not know any little boy in the world who is happier than yours, Iliapa,' Missus would sometimes say to her. 'He is so jolly all the time; when he is playing with his grandfather, when he listens to you telling him your old Aunt Labea's stories of the long-ago, and when he gets on horse-back and rides with his father, holding the reins like a little man.'

By the time that Alibaka was six years old, he had learned to ride by himself. Not only so, but he would catch Tim by the mane, lead him to the fence of the stock-paddock, and there, getting upon the rails, put the bridle on him, and ride him barebacked round the paddock at a gentle canter. Tim, of course, was a very quiet old horse, who had done so much work in his day, that he had now very little to do, except to feed quietly where the grass was softest, stand in the shade of the box- or gum-trees when the sun was hot, and go at a gentle pace to drive other horses into the stock-yard, when they were wanted. Yet no matter how quiet a horse may be, it was a feat for a little boy of six to be able to fix a bridle on his head and ride him barebacked.

The blacks talked of this far and near, so that when any of them came to Balkara who were strangers to the place, almost the first thing they said was, 'Where is the little boy who is such a clever rider?' And not only the blacks, but white people also, came to hear of the wonderful little 'jockey,' as he came to be called, and used to ask to see him go through the little play of catching a horse, fixing a bridle on his head, and riding him barebacked.

Alibaka's eighth birthday was a specially happy one. Missus gave him on this day, a small saddle that had once belonged to her son Bob, who was now a big lad away at college. Alibaka's joy was beyond words, and when that afternoon he rode out with his father, with his little saddle, on a young grey pony called Dick, to say that he was as happy as a king would be really short of the truth. For where is the king who has all that he wants in this world, and is quite free from care and from sorrow? Iliapa and Erungara looked after the father and son as they rode away, and were almost as much delighted as the little man himself. Four months later an event took place that strangely affected the life of this little aboriginal family.

It was a warm night in November. Alibaka was asleep, while his father and mother and Erungara sat at the door of the little slab hut that had been put up for Nalbuka close to the horse-paddock which was his special charge. Erungara was telling the young people how he had at one time seen many white men in the valley of the Jimarra Creek, making holes in the ground and digging up out of the dirt lumps of the heavy yellow stuff that they make into shining buttons and call money. 'And with this stuff that they pick out of the dirt, they can get sheep and horses and cows; clothes and blankets and houses and big stations like Roalmah and Balkara. They are a queer people – sometimes wise and sometimes very silly,' added Erungara thoughtfully.

While he was speaking, Nalbuka started up, looking hard towards the native camp.

'There are two black men coming up,' he said, 'by this side of the Balkara.' In a general way the blacks go about very little at night. This made Nalbuka wonder who they were and what they were after. When they came into full view in the moonlight they stood still looking around, as if not sure which way they should take.

'Are you looking for me?' cried Nalbuka, speaking in the native tongue.

'Yes, yes. Nalbuka, they told me at the camp you were on this side of the river,' replied one of the men, as they both came rapidly towards the little group in front of the hut.'

'Maleka,' cried Nalbuka in a tone of wonder.

'Yes, Maleka and his son Nanka, that was lost so long,' said Maleka, putting his hand proudly on the shoulder of the tall young man who was with him, dressed from head to foot in well-fitting garments.

There were cries of surprise and joy and welcome. But when offers of food and drink were made, Nanka said, 'We ate well at sunset; we have much to tell you and no time to lose.'

'You will eat when your talk is over,' said Iliapa, slipping into the hut. Then the four men sat down in a circle and Nanka told his tale.

'You know I have been long, long away from all my own people,' he said. 'A police trooper took me to Alice Springs, then away to the Northern Territory. For many years I have been a tracker to the police force. I am now, but not in uniform. I am on what they call secret service. They gave me the name of being one of the most cunning trackers in Australia. When the inspector of police wants to find things out from the blacks, he will sometimes say, "You may as well tell me what really took place, for we have a tracker here, as you know, who can become the very shadow of a guilty man. He may then go to the left or to the right, to the north, south, east or west; he may lie in a cave, or climb a mountain to the sky; he may hide among the rushes round a swamp, or go far by the Great Salt Water that has only one shore; but Jim – that is what they call me – will find him. Jim can track a spider or a bullock, a man or a lizard, even on horseback, running all the time, hardly looking at the ground." After a time they sent me sometimes all alone as far as Queensland and New South Wales to find out about men who were thought to have done some evil thing. I have been sent here in that way. I will tell you why. Some moons ago an inspector of police came on a visit from

Adelaide. One day he got a letter from a brother who looks after the men that are in prison all their lives. One of these is a boundary-rider of Roalmah, who was tried some years ago for killing a black man one night at the Wonka Creek.'

At these words Nalbuka started as if to rise to his feet, but Erungara put a warning hand on his shoulder and Jim went on as if he saw nothing.

'The boundary-man paid a very clever man of law to speak for him, so he was not hung, only kept all the time in prison. Now a brother who lived far away in the west and did not know what happened to the boundary-man, has died and left him more money than can be counted, that he got out of a gold mine. The inspector's brother wrote in the letter that the boundary-man is quite certain there was a black man standing over Ingunta when he was killed; and that a big bag of gold was waiting for the man who could find out who that black man was. When the inspector was a trooper at Roalmah he always knew how to find things out about the blacks; but when he had a bad fall and had to go away, the one who was in his place was stupid and would not believe the boundary-rider, so no search was made.'

'So now you have come for the black man who stood over Ingunta, so that he may be put in prison in place of the boundary-rider, who has so much gold to give away when he gets out,' cried Nalbuka, standing up at his full height, with a fierce light in his eyes.

'No, no no; that is not so,' said Erungara, standing up beside Nalbuka with his hand on his arm.

'Can you think that I would bring my son to you for such a reason?' asked Maleka, more sorry than angry.

'Sit down, Nalbuka, and let me finish my story,' said Jim in a calm friendly voice. 'Yes, that was why the inspector sent me on a strong horse that was changed for another on the way down. "Go among all the blacks of the district," he said; "track with your mind in the way that you track with your eyes and your feet. First of all, go to your own people, as if you had just come only to see them. Do not tell a soul that you are working for the police. You know how to find things out without asking a string of questions." The first I went to were my father and my mother. That was two days ago. The night I found them, my father and I spoke together till it was getting red in the east. There was so much to say. Without a word or a sign from me he told me all about you and what took place at Wonka Creek. We did not lose one hour in coming to you. For hear me, Nalbuka. You must leave before it can ever be said or thought that you went away because I came.'

'Will not the station blacks at our camp here know that you came to-night?' asked Nalbuka.

'Oh, no; I did not go near the camp. I hid in a safe place when my father went to ask for you. He will stay with Erungara for some days. Before there is light enough in the sky to tell a white cockatoo from a crow, we two must steal away. You know how to get to Colloolloo on the way to the Big Ranges, without touching the mail track. I will go with you half a day, you will ride my horse and I can ride him back.'

'Your horse? But he is not here,' said Erungara.

'Not where you can see him,' said Jim, smiling. Then, turning to Nalbuka, he went on:

'I know the manager of Colloolloo, he will be glad to give you work till I go back to the Northern Territory. You can return with me and stay there till all danger is over. That will not be till the inspector makes search for himself by coming to the district.'

'The Master of Balkara has been very good to us,' said Erungara. 'Should not Nalbuka see him before he goes away?'

'Not at all,' replied Jim. 'Nalbuka might tell him from now till the sun is high and the white man would not see how it could be.

'"I went to touch Ingunta for death. I stood over my enemy and let the stone fall, when I picked it up it was covered with his blood" – that is the story that the white man would drag out of him.'

All this time Nalbuka was strangely silent.

'You agree with our plan?' said Nanka with a half-puzzled look.

'I do not agree to go flying away like a man that has spilled blood. You, Maleka, will never open your lips to tell how I stood by Ingunta before his body was cold. There is no one else who knows.'

Maleka hung his head; his lips moved as if he were going to speak. But only a low moan broke the stillness. Nalbuka looked at him with angry suspicion.

'You did not keep your promise,' he said harshly.

Maleka looked up, and the tears were streaming down his cheeks.

'A few moons ago I was ill. My head burned, and my words were the words of one who does not know his right hand from his left. "Tell me again that strange story about Nalbuka, when he went to touch Ingunta for death, and found him already dead," my wife said to me one day when my sickness was gone. When I asked her if she had told anyone, she said yes. . . .'

'And now it is known to all the Camp of Roalmah,' said Nalbuka slowly. He realized at once the danger that hung over him.

'My mother is old and blind; when Roalmah blacks come to see her she speaks to them of all the things she knows,' said Nanka. 'But she had no thought of doing you any harm. And no harm would come – only that much gold has been left to the man in prison, and the inspector is hungry and thirsty to get some of it.'

'Should we start at once?' asked Nalbuka, standing up with the set face of a man who has to flee for his life.

Iliapa had made food ready; the men ate and drank before lying down. In a few hours Nalbuka and Jim rose silently while it was dark save for the myriads of stars that filled the sky.

'I will come back as soon as I can and find you here all right,' were Nalbuka's last words to Iliapa. He would not allow her to wake up Alibaka to say good-bye. Perhaps he was afraid that the little clinging arms might set the tears flowing that it was so hard to keep back. As it was, he showed nothing of the keen desolation that filled his mind in going back to the old lonely wandering life far from his young wife and his happy boy.

CHAPTER 8

Four years passed away and still Nalbuka did not come back. Several times during those years they got tidings of him through drovers dealing between Roalmah and other stations and the Northern Territory. The messages were given to the Master of Roalmah for Maleka and were always the same: 'Nanka and his cousin are well.' Erungara would often say, 'Nalbuka does not stay away because he does not want to come back. He stays because it would not be yet safe for him to return. When it is safe, he will come to us. That will be a joyful day for us all.'

Iliapa rested on this belief. Having her boy and her father to care for, being very kindly treated by the Balkara people, with work that she liked to do, as well as plenty of time for herself, she did not fret nor give way to gloomy thoughts. But Alibaka was sometimes very restless and almost unhappy.'

'Why did father go away?' This was the great mystery that cast a shadow on his little life, ever since he woke up in the cloudless dawn of a November morning to find his father gone. The world since then had not seemed to him quite the same place. Not that he became a sad or discontented boy. Far from it. He was as a rule full of play and energy. He was a great mimic and learned to imitate the notes of birds and the cries of the wild creatures of the woods with wonderful skill. The cooing notes of the wood-pigeon, the carols of the magpie, the fairy-like tinkling of the little blue wren, the jirr-jirr of the grey and black fantail – these and the songs and cries of other birds that were to be heard on the banks of the Balkara, he picked up like his mother-tongue. Often when he came back from riding on errands and other light work that he was trusted to do, he loved to hide himself somewhere near his grandfather and make a little concert of birds singing long and loud till Erungara would peer up into the sky and say, 'Where can all these birds be, that are singing away like this?' Then Alibaka would laugh merrily and say the birds had gone away, but he had come to stay.

At other times he would come home a very silent boy with a grave face. Then his mother and grandfather knew that something had made him think of his father, and that his mind was full of the old questioning – 'Why did he go away and when will he come back?' At such times they would make up cheerful little stories of Nalbuka's return. It might be in the early morning, or at sunset or when the moon was riding high among the stars. Alibaka would soon join in, one detail after another being added till the home-coming was made into the plot of quite a number of joyful little dramas. The one that Alibaka liked best and that was largely built up by his own eager little imagination was that of a messenger coming to say, 'Your father is sitting down at such a place. He has come a long way and is very tired. He wants you to come and meet him. You see, Nandi, you could not leave grandfather, and he is too old to come on a journey. So I would go alone with the messenger. I would ride Cossack and go fast – oh, so fast to Batja.'

Here Iliapa would take up the tale and tell how she would have a big meal ready for father and son when they came, and how Batja would have many tales to tell them of what he saw and did at the Great Salt Water. Erungara would end the story by saying that at last when all danger was over, Batja would tell them why he had to leave Balkara at an hour's notice and had to stay away so long.

All this pleased Alibaka immensely. It was not like wild stories of long-ago, with a rain-bird turning into a Jew-lizard, a man carrying the moon on his pitchie to look for witchetty grubs, people going down under the ground, and up into the sky, sometimes fighting each other with lightning and thunder. No, father's home-coming, riding to meet him, and all the rest would be real. There was nothing at all in the story that was not quite possible. But sometimes we have to find out that the possible is a cunning sort of witch, that has the power of turning from softly lisping waves into walls of adamant.

It was on Alibaka's twelfth birthday that the home-coming story reached its final form. A few weeks later several black men came from Roalmah on their way to a corroboree at a place forty miles beyond Balkara. Among them was Yukuta. Very soon after getting to the blacks' camp, he found his way to the mia-mia that Erungara had near Nalbuka's hut, that was still occupied by Iliapa and her boy. Erungara greeted the new-comer in his usual kindly way, but Yukuta said in an angry voice:

'You used to be an Oknirabata of the Arunta Nation. A great teacher of the old laws and the old customs; but since you began giving magic sticks and stones for killing, you no longer keep your promise according to the old laws.'

Erungara looked at the speaker with troubled eyes. The first part of his speech he did not mind. He knew Yukuta, like so many others, would not understand his views of magic. But to be accused of not keeping his promise according to the old laws touched him keenly.

'You are using false and foolish words,' he said sternly. 'What promise of mine has ever been broken?'

'You promised your daughter Iliapa to me in marriage, and yet you gave her to another man.'

Erungara looked for a moment at Yukuta in silence, then said slowly: 'You are like the man who put barbs on his spear to kill a shadow. It was you who sent a message to me that you were going far away, and that you no longer wished for my daughter.'

'Yes, but what were the rude and saucy words that you sent to me, before you got my message?'

Erungara leant his head on his hand for a moment or two in deep thought. He was getting feeble, and his memory was weak, so that it was easy to confuse him. But in a short time he said in a firm voice: 'I sent no message at all to you – not a word. It was ever my way to keep my promise in all things. I never broke the old laws, or went away from the old customs. Only went back to some ancient ones that had been forgotten.'

'Yet the mocking words were given to me as if from your lips. "If you want a wife, seek one out who is old enough to be the mother of my daughter. She must be given to one who is young and strong with a good temper, not one who is ugly with the temper of a snake."'

On hearing these words the look that came into Erungara's face was nothing short of horror. Chiefly because to go back on his word and break a sacred law seemed to him a most grave offence. But also because he was on the whole kindly and courteous – ways that his position as a teacher and medicine man had made into a second nature.

'Labea's words,' he murmured, bowing his head in shame, while tears rolled down his cheeks. Yukuta, who was a very cunning old rascal and had his own ends to serve by making as much as possible of the wrong done to him, said in a tone of wonder:

'But how do you come to let your sister – a weak old woman – come between you and the fixed laws of long-ago?'

Erungara groaned aloud, rocking himself to and fro, an image of forlorn distress.

'Let her?' he repeated in a voice little above a whisper. For this blow had brought on the great weakness and dizzy feeling that had troubled him since the time he had been so badly wounded. 'You might as well ask me how I let the thunder roll in the sky, and spinifex hurt the naked skin.'

At this moment Iliapa came in sight coming from the Big House with a basket on her arm, Alibaka bounding by her side. He was tall for his age and well-formed, with a pleasant face and a smile for every one. Yukuta looked at the boy with greedy eyes, while he greeted the mother with a playful nickname.

'Have you brought bad news to my father?' she said coldly, seeing his cheeks still wet with tears and knowing of old that Yukuta had no gift for carrying glad tidings.

'Some words that were made up by his sister Labea seem to him very bad news,' said Yukuta, with a laugh in which there was no mirth.

At once Iliapa knew that her father was in trouble because he had been deceived by the message sent to and fro by her aunt. Fearing he might question her, she made haste to give him the tea and cake she always brought to him in the afternoon. No native will eat without asking a visitor to join him. So she placed a pannikin of sugared tea and a portion of cake before each, saying, 'I must run back now – Missus is waiting for me to finish some sewing.' Alibaka went with her, but when he was a few yards away Yukuta called him back. Opening the large wallet, or native portmanteau, which all black men carry with them when going to corroborees or tribal ceremonies, he toolk out of it a pretty shell, called Lonka-lonka, saying, 'Keep this till I see you again.'

Alibaka was delighted, for it was a rare shell, and when held up in the sunlight made a little rainbow of dazzling colours.

'You hardly remember your father – it is so long since he went away,' Yukuta said when the boy thanked him.

'Oh yes, I do, quite well. He may come back any time. One day a messenger may come and tell us he is on the way – perhaps sitting down somewhere, tired of the long journey from the Great Salt Water. Then I will go to meet him on a fast horse.'

Alibaka, with a happy smile on his face, ran to catch up his mother, without waiting for any more talk.

'That would be one way of getting him,' said Yukuta to himself.

Turning to Erungara, he said, 'Do you know why I gave him that pretty shell? I gave it to him as a spell that makes it quite sure he will before long come away with me.'

'Go away with you? Your words are dark to me,' said Erungara. But though they might be dark, they filled him with fear; his voice trembled and the hand in which he held his pannikin shook so that some of the tea was spilt. There was something snake-like in the intent vicious look in Yukuta's small bright eyes as he watched every look and movement of the old medicine man.

'Hear me, Erungara, once a great teacher of the Arunta people. The young ones may be careless of the old ways. But you and I know that if we do not keep to the laws of long-ago, bad things will happen to us. Where is now the man to whom you gave your daughter, though she was promised to me when she was at her mother's breast? Yes, he may come back or he may not. It is many summers since he left you.'

'It was never my way to forget the old laws or to break my promise,' said Erungara, shaken with misery, almost sobbing as he spoke, while tears again ran down his cheeks.

'Yet you have done me great evil by heeding the words of an old woman who was ever my enemy. Why did you not say to her, "Yukuta is a good man – Yukuta keeps to the old laws"? But do not weep, Erungara. There is a way in which you can make up for the wrong you did me and keep more harm from coming on yourself. Was it not one of the old laws that if a woman was promised to one man and taken by another, if she had a son he might be given to the first man?'

'Hear me, Erungara,' continued Yukuta, raising his strong, thick voice, as the poor old man dashed away his tears and made an effort to speak. 'Hear me and mark my words. The boy has no father and you are very old and very feeble. Alibaka should soon be made one of the young men of the tribe. Here he would become as a cat that is so tame that he forgets how to run up a tree, how to kill a bird, or even catch a mouse. So tame and foolish that he will squeal out with fear at the shadow of a dingo. Give him to me if only for a time and I will be to him as a father. You will think of this till I come back from

Okalparra, when the last half of this moon has gone. Say no word of our plan to Iliapa. I will know how to get Alibaka away without letting her make any noise or asking what she thinks about the matter. When was it the way of our people to heed a woman as if she were one to do more than what she is told?' Yukuta spoke with the scorn of a man who knows that the best way to rule women is with the help of a good stout waddy.

It was about a fortnight after this when Yukuta and the other black men came back from Okalparra a little after the sun had set. His companions went to the native camp on the Balkara, but Yukuta left them when the Big House came in sight and went direct towards the horse-paddock to the slab hut. When he drew near it he stood stock-still with a bewildered look. For a moment he could not believe his eyes. Erungara's mia-mia was gone. Not a trace of it was left. But yes – there was a sign – a wide circle where fire had burned, and where ashes had been carefully swept away. Erungara was dead! If he had only gone away for a time his mia-mia would not have been burnt. After all, it was as well he was out of the way. It might be easier now to get hold of that boy. He heard a low hissing cry. Turning round he stood face to face with Iliapa.

But what had come over the girl? Her face was so full of anger and hate that Yukuta drew back, fearing she might spring at his throat like a wild cat mad with pain. But though she would like to have seen him dead at her feet, she knew that her slender hands could do him no harm.

'So you came to make sure that my father is dead,' she said, trembling with fury. 'Yes, yes, you killed him. He was old and weak and you brought back the trouble to his head. He lived only four days after he saw your wicked face, and heard your hateful tongue. Oh, I did wrong to leave you here alone with him. I should have taken the wild bulldog off the chain and made him tear you to pieces.'

No one had ever before heard Iliapa speak like this, or seen her so carried away with rage. Usually she was gentle almost to meekness. But human creatures capable of great love have in them a depth of passion that will at times sweep all before it like a flood. There was a dangerous malice in Yukuta's face as he listened almost in silence. When at last he began to speak, Iliapa raised both hands, saying: 'Go – go out of my sight – creature unfit to be looked at – unfit to be touched.'

This took place on Monday. On the following Thursday Alibaka was sent with a message to some men who were working at what was known as the Ten Mile Dam. When the overseer sent him he told him, if there was anything he could do to help, he might stay till Saturday; but to be sure to ride back by noon on that day.

'What can be keeping that boy of ours?' he said to Iliapa at three o'clock on Saturday afternoon, as she sat working a sewing-machine on the veranda of the store-room. She did not know that he was to be back by a certain hour, and learning that he was so much behind time, an uneasy feeling came over her. She closed the machine, and walked across to the Big House. This with its out-buildings was on a rise, which gave a good view of the surrounding country. She went past the stables, towards the Balkara, straining her eyes in the direction of the Ten Mile Dam. A horseman came in sight. She watched eagerly, till the rider was near enough for her to see that he was one of the station hands. 'I will go and ask him if he saw anything of Nalbuka,' she thought. At that moment a man came out from the thicket of box shrubs by which Iliapa stood.

It was Yukuta.

'Where is my boy? What have you done to him?' Her voice shook with terror, when she saw the fiendish joy in his small eyes.

'I have walked a long way with a message for you, also that I might see you tremble with fear, that I might hear you beg me to speak to you in place of saying, "Go out of my sight – creature unfit to be looked at, unfit to be touched." Yes, are you shaking like dry grass in a high wind – you want me not to go out of your sight but to tell you about your boy. The white man that has him now wants you to tell the Master that the horse your boy was riding, with the saddle and bridle, will be brought here to-morrow by one of the black boys of Roalmah.'

'Are you telling me lies or are you not? Alibaka is a big strong boy; he is not a fool – why should he go away with a stranger?'

Now that the first shock was over, Iliapa's mind was clearer. She knew that if Yukuta had really hurt her boy, he would not have dared to come near Balkara. If she could only find out where Alibaka was, or keep Yukuta talking till some one came near who would help her. She saw that he had a gun which he had placed against one of the shrubs and that he kept looking along the river from time to time as if to guard against being taken by surprise.

'You would be locked up if the police saw you with a gun. You did not have it when you were here before. Who gave it to you?' asked

Iliapa, the thought coming suddenly into her mind that it was given by the man who had taken her boy away.

Yukuta laughed wickedly. 'Often when people ask many questions none of them get a reply,' he said, glancing as he spoke towards the river. Two black men were walking along the bank on their way to the camp. Yukuta at once glided back into the midst of the shrubs where he was hidden from sight. Iliapa looked past the stables to the Big House. And there, standing midway between the buildings, she saw a sight that made her heart beat as if it had got into her throat. It was the Master of Balkara in talk with a police trooper in full uniform. It went through her mind in a flash that she could make use of this to frighten Yukuta into telling her where Alibaka was, and how he came to go away with a stranger. She knew the trooper had come about some cattle that had been stolen from a distant part of the run. But she knew, too, that it was said by some of the natives in the camp that Yukuta had fled from the station to which he had gone, near the Great Salt Water, because of some evil deed he had done there.

When the two black men on the bank of the river were out of sight, Yukuta came from his hiding-place. Iliapa had shifted her position a little, so that she stood more directly between him and the two men who were still in close talk.

'Will you tell me where my boy is now, and how he came to go with a stranger?' she said, speaking in a calm voice, though she panted like one who has been running for some time.

'He went with the white man because the white man told him his father had sent for him,' replied Yukuta, laughing as if at a good joke. 'Told him his father was a journey of two suns away, where he had to sit down because he was too ill to travel. But where your boy has been taken – that I will not tell you.'

'Did you know that a police trooper was looking for you?' said Iliapa, standing aside, and pointing in his direction. Yukuta stepped from the shelter of the shrub by which he stood. When he saw the Master of Balkara and the trooper so near, he gave a hoarse little cry like an animal that has been suddenly trapped. Then he caught up his gun and netted bag and wallet, as if to dash away.

'Don't move or I will call out,' said Iliapa in a stern voice. 'His saddled horse is in the stable, his loaded little gun is on his hip. He could shoot you down, or catch you before you got near the river. He will tie your hands and lock you up for what you did at Mindano.' Yukuta, retreating behind the shrubs, glared at her for a moment in silence. Then he spoke: 'If you call out and let me taken, who will tell you where Alibaka is going? Hear me, Iliapa, daughter of Erungara, if you do not lift a finger against me, I will tell you.'

As Yukuta spoke, great drops of sweat rolled down his face. Through the shrubs he could see the men who were so near that one cry would bring them to the spot before he could get fifty yards away.

'Tell me – I will not lift a finger against you,' said Iliapa. There was a strange ringing in her ears. She heard Yukuta speaking as if he were far away. It was to Labalama that the white man took Alibaka. Long ago, Simon – that was the man's name – had heard much talk of Alibaka being a great rider and clever with horses. Long ago he had said to Yukuta: 'If you bring me that boy, I will give you a gun, two good knives and a great deal of tobacco.' On the day after Iliapa was mad because her father died, Yukuta met Simon on the way to Roalmah. Simon was in the district buying horses. He said: 'I will camp on the Balkara some miles away from the Big House, till you bring me word where I can meet the boy alone.' Now they are on the way to Labalama. I have told you the truth, for you will not raise a finger against me or speak a word to do me harm.

Yukuta glided away, making no more noise than a lizard. But Iliapa lay down under the shrubs. She had thought of Alibaka being as far away as Jimarra Creek or Roalmah. But Labalama – that was to her like the other end of the world. Would she ever see him again? Her father was dead, Nalbuka was gone more seasons than she could count. Now, worse than all, her boy was stolen from her. She lay stone-still, unable to shed a tear.

CHAPTER 9

Iliapa slept heavily for hours. When she awoke a few stars were coming out, and a moon, newly born as the natives say, was hanging like a glimmering crescent of silver in the violet sky. When Iliapa got to the Big House, Missus and Helen met her on the veranda.

'Oh, Iliapa, where have you been? We have looked for you everywhere. At last I thought that you, too, had gone away without saying a word. Do you know that Alibaka has gone away with some man who is taking him to his father? Bill, the boundary-rider, met them on Friday. The Master was very cross when he got the news.'

Iliapa listened with a dazed look. But at the last words her eyes flashed, and she said in a hard voice: 'The Master heard big one lie; me want to see him and tell him.'

'He has gone away for two or three days to Yulta with the police trooper. But what do you mean, Iliapa, by "big one lie"?'

Iliapa told her story as well as she could. Then she sat and sobbed as if her heart would break. When she calmed down, Helen brought her some tea and comforted her as best she could.

'You will be better after you have slept,' Missus said, bringing her a rug to lie on the veranda, where she would not be so lonely.

'Sleep till the sun is up, Iliapa' said Helen, 'then we will see what we can do.'

But long before the sun was up there was a tapping at Helen's open window. On going to see who could want her in the early dawn, there was Iliapa ready for a journey.

'Tell Missus when she get up, me gone after my boy,' she said. 'Don't tell her till I be away – she would say, "It is too far, you be mad." But I must go – I must go.'

Helen, of course, went to call her mother. There was something of terror in the mother's face, when she saw Iliapa with her bundle, her basket and water-bag, ready to set out on a tramp of over two hundred miles through tracks of sand and spinifex, and stretches of waterless country. For Missus knew a great deal of the natives, and she understood the set look on the black woman's face. The look of one whose mind has closed down on a single purpose and can no more be moved than an iron lock that is fastened with a strong key. She felt it was all but hopeless to beg Iliapa even to delay this wild journey. But she made the effort.

'At least wait till the Master comes back – he will know how to help you.'

'I must go – I must, I must. Me cannot wait.'

'Last night you were reasonable,' said Helen. 'When I said that Alibaka was a strong, sensible boy, you said he would come back, when he found that the white man did not take him to his father. Do tell me, Iliapa, if anything happened since then to make you leave us, and go away all alone. I could cry like a baby to think of you – hungry and thirsty in the desert, with no one to help you.' The tears came thick into Helen's eyes as she spoke.

'Yes, me tell you; in the night, my boy cry – he cry an' he call me to come to him. He want me. To-day me must go.'

There was no break in her voice, or any outward sign of grief. She was so bent on the task before her that all weakness was kept in the background. Mother and daughter felt that further entreaty was useless. They were as if faced by something overruled by fate.

'Well, Iliapa – you faithful little soul,' said Missus, stroking Iliapa's cheek as she spoke. 'If we cannot keep you from going, we can at least drive you a stage on the way to Labalama. Go and have something to eat while we dress and get breakfast.'

'If only there was some other black woman or girl to go with her,' said Helen as she poured out the tea.

'If poor old Norah were a few years younger, she would be the very one,' said her mother. Then they went over one after one of the native women who were at Balkara or in the neighbourhood. But this one was too lazy, and another too young; one was too fat and another ill-tempered, this one had not pluck enough, and that one was not fit for other reasons, while two or three had young children.

'I'll tell you what, mother,' said Helen at last; 'let us go as far as Antaka. We have long owed them a visit, and the Brownes would be only too glad to help if they have anyone that would suit.'

'A very good plan, my dear – I am glad you thought of it,' replied her mother; 'it will be thirty-six miles off the terrible tramp to Labalama. Mrs Browne was there six months or so back. She may know of some one who can help Iliapa – if the poor dear ever gets there.'

In less than an hour they started for Antaka in a light American buggy, with a pair of horses that Helen was used to driving. They were fresh and the track was good through level well-wooded country, so that they got over the thirty-six miles in a little over four hours. Fortune favoured them. As they drew near the native camp, within half a mile of the Head Station, one called out 'Coo-ee, Coo-ee' in a jubilant voice and came running to meet them. 'It be Polde,' cried Iliapa joyfully, for they were always good friends and it was long since they had seen each other.

'Go to her, Iliapa, and tell her your story,' said Missus. 'The very one of all others, if she will only take it in her head to go,' she added, as the two met with cries of joy from Polde.

'Oh, how lucky – if only she will,' said Helen. 'She is so strong and lively – she can climb trees like a 'possum, run like an emu, and kill game like the men who do nothing but hunt. It takes very little, I know, to make her angry or to make her cry. But she gets over it in a minute and laughs while the tears are on her cheeks.'

'Yes, and being such a free lance, never long in one place, she must know the country from A to Z,' rejoined her mother.

In a very short time the two came running up to the trap breathless with excitement. Polde had at once offered to go with her friend, and the gladness in Iliapa's face showed what a boon the offer was. Another thing that heartened her was the news that her long-lost sister, Nabata, was in or near Labalama.

'Me bin all the way to Labalama two o' 'ree time,' explained Polde. 'My coolie he die there las' year.'

'I am sorry to hear that,' said Missus, more moved by politeness than regret, feeling sure that Polde's brief married life was likely to be a stormy episode.

'Me not sorry,' Polde shook her head emphatically as she spoke. 'He big one, old all the time and often a good bit cranky. Now me go an' get baske' an' bag an' all fings ready an' come along.'

The story of Iliapa and her boy made a great stir in the Browne household. They all agreed that Iliapa could have no better mate than Polde for the perilous trek to Labalama. Each one thught of something to help in that gret adventure. Mrs Browne wrote a letter to her friend, Dr Grey, that Iliapa would give him as soon as she got there. Dick, the only boy at home, helped his younger sister to make up packets of tea and sugar and large biscuits, and half a leg of newly-cooked mutton. They would have added many more things, but they were restrained by the need of keeping down the weight that each must carry.

The elder girl aided the governess to run up a skirt and blouse for Polde, of the same kind that Iliapa wore, a dark-blue jean, so strong as to be almost untearable. Mr Browne got out an outline map of the country they would go through.

'The worst part for them,' he said, 'will be the Red Sand Desert. But if they get on fairly well, a day or two after they get over this, they should meet Hussein. From Labalama to the Desert all travellers keep pretty close to the Overland Telegraph Line; so if they are on the look-out they won't miss him. I'll give them a message for him and he will give them any help in his power.'

Hussein was an Afghan in charge of a party with camels bringing goods to the inland stations from Labalama, to which trains came every second week from Adelaide. Hussein could write and read a little English. Mr Browne wrote in a large clear hand, 'Balkara and Antaka want you to help these two native women in any way you can.' This was put into a very strong envelope and securely fastened to Iliapa's basket. The letter to Dr Grey was put in a little black silken bag, fastened with a tape to tie round her neck for safe keeping. 'Now mind, Iliapa,' said Mrs Browne. 'The first thing you do when you get to Labalama is to go to Dr Grey's house – anyone will show you where it is – and give this letter into his own hands. Be sure not to give it to anyone else. If he is not in when you get there, keep it until he comes.'

So when everything was ready for the two, who were to get away by the break of day, they said good-bye to their friends and went to sleep in Polde's mia-mia. But when they were ready to go at the first streak of dawn, there was Dick calling to them to come up to the Big House. Here there was some breakfast ready for them, and there was Helen and one of the Browne girls with two of the Antaka horses harnessed to the buggy. 'We are going to drive you as far as the Early Camp Creek for good luck,' they said.

It was a little beyond the creek where they waved the last good-byes, as the two set out southward on the track to Labalama, which here lay over a fine stretch of country. Iliapa had not a word to say as they went on at a good swinging pace. Polde laughed and chattered in high spirits, and finding her mate so silent, she chanted a stave in a blithe voice, from a corroboree chant of the Adelaide natives:

Miny-el-ity yarluke an-ambe
Aly-el-arr, yerk-in yangaiak-ar.

CHAPTER 10

An hour after mid-day, when the sun was at its hottest, they rested in the shade of some box-trees, made a quart pot of tea, and ate some biscuits. After that they both slept, and when they woke up, the sun was slanting to the west, and the wind was cooler. They went on their way much refreshed, and walked so well, tht at sunset they reached what was known as the Platypus Spring, where the water was quite cold, and clear as glass.

'We have come more than a big-day's journey,' said Polde, joyfully, 'and yet we are not tired. Soon, soon we rise one morning and go on, and then in one moment we stop. What is that we see? One and two and three, and many smokes of a black-fellow camp, spreading out close to the ground; no, they are tall and thin. They are the smokes of Labalama – of Labalama, where Alibaka, the son of Iliapa, sits down. Alibaka . . . '

Polde stopped all at once and stared at Iliapa, as if she could not believe her eyes. For there was the mother of Alibaka, who should be so full of joy at the words she heard, with the tears running down her cheeks like rain.

'Ah, Polde,' she said brokenly, 'you make me afraid. If the white man that took away my boy, went to another place, and not to Labalama at all – if he put him on a wild horse, and the horse ran away . . . '

'Yes, and if a bird flew down from the sky and picked off all his hair; if a fly jumped on his face and flew off with his nose; if a little black ant crawled out of a hole, and gobbled up his toes.'

Polde went on making up all sorts of absurd things, until she made Iliapa laugh. For all that, now when the uplift of getting away was over, fears which she could not keep back, crowded into the mother's mind.

After they had eaten, they lay down, and watched the stars come out; neither of them was sleepy, and as Iliapa was so silent, Polde said, 'Would you like to hear the story of the Great One, that is told by the Little Hawk People?'

Iliapa said that she would very much, so Polde, who as long as she was awake, could not bear silence, settled herself comfortably.

'The first time that the Great One came down from the sun to the earth, he was very thirsty, so he looked for a creek with a big water-hole. He found a skull near it and drank up the water until there was only a mouthful left. But this mouthful held a frog, a tadpole, and a small egg, that was so young it had not half done growing.

'Then the Great One looked for a lake with fish, and he caught so many of them that they lay in a heap as big as a hill.'

'Did he have a net?' asked Iliapa.

'No. He had a long spear, and every time he stuck it in the water, there was a fine fat fish, and the Great One threw it over his shoulder on the ground. Then he stuck the spear again, and got another fish as fast as you can wink an eye. At last there was no fish left in the lake, but a tiny one that was so young, it had grown only a tail as thick as a blade of grass.

'So the Great One said, "You are so small that I could not roast you, nor taste you on my tongue. Stay there till you get a fat tail so that you make coals sing when you are cooked for eating."

'The tiny fish, that was so small it had grown a tail only as big as a blade of grass, laughed a small laugh, like the sound of a grasshopper jumping on a dry blade of grass. He went to the far side of the lake asking three flies to come with him, and make a corrobboree, because he was too small to be put on the coals and eaten.

'"Now I will make a fire and roast the fish and eat, till the sun has to run over the ground again, to get back to the east in time to make it morning," said the Great One, looking at the hill of fish that he had fished out of the lake. He sat down to rub his grass-sticks to make a fire. But when he looked into his basket the sticks for making a fire were not there.

'"I must have dropped them by the water-hole, where I drank all the water, except the mouthful which holds a frog, a tadpole and a small egg that has not done growing," said the Great One. He ran to the water-hole so fast that he left the wind far behind him. But nothing was there as he left it.

'"Get out of the water," said the frog to the tadpole, as soon as the

Great One had gone away, "for there will not be enough for me and my tribe, when my mate comes back."

'"My tail is so thin, it takes up no room at all," replied the tadpole, "and as for my head, I can keep it quite out of the water, so that I shall not be in the way, even of the smallest of your tribe. The one that takes up so much room is the egg, and when he gets older it may be worse – for you never know what is going to come out of an egg. It may be something that will eat a frog and a tadpole at one mouthful, and then cry for more. I will help you to push him out. When your mate comes back there will be plenty of room for your tribe. You can then make a corrobboree, and eat me if you like."

'"What you say about the egg is true," said the frog. "We must get him out first, and then I will see about you afterwards."

'When the tadpole heard this, he went some distance away, and stayed there looking at the frog and the egg to see what would happen. The frog puffed out his stomach, made his neck big, swelled his eyes and spread out his claws, and rolled the egg up the bank of the creek. But when it was almost at the top, it turned over and rolled back again, and lay in the water as before.

'"You said you would help me push the egg away, but there you play around in the water, and leave me to do all the work," said the frog, getting very angry at the tadpole.

'"I am doing two things," replied the tadpole; "keeping my head out of the water, as I promised you, and taking care that the Great One does not come to drink you up. That is the way I help you, and no one can do more than two things at a time. Try again and do not speak. You will want all your breath to get that egg up the bank, and safe out of your way. You will be sorry if the shell opens, and something comes out that eats a frog at one mouthful, and then cries for more."

'"I would rather push you out first," said the frog, his eyes bobbing from side to side with rage. "You are growing faster than the egg. Your tail-end is getting more like a bag than a tail."

'"You ought to be glad, there will be something more for you to eat, when your mate comes back, and your tribe is starving," said the tadpole, going away from the frog as far as he could, and standing on his head, in place of keeping it out of the water, as he had said. Once more the frog puffed out his stomach, made his neck thick, swelled his eyes, spread out his claws, and shoved the egg up the bank, giving it such a push at the top, that it rolled away into a clump of spear-grass.

'When the frog got back into the water, he was so tired that in one wink he fell asleep under the rushes, and snored so loud that a cross old platypus woke up, and turned his wife out of her hole, in the bank of the creek, for making such a noise.

'The egg lay quite still in the grass and a blue dove came flying overhead. When she saw the egg she gave coos and coos of joy.

'"My egg that I lost two moons ago. My own dear egg with the little green spots all over it," said the blue dove. She flew down and folded her wings and sat on the egg, meaning to hatch it day and night. She closed her eyes and was very happy. But in a short time the Great One came running back, looking for his grass-sticks to make a fire, and stumbled on the clump of spear-grass in which the blue dove was hatching her egg. She spread out her wings in a fright, and flew up to the sky to be safe. Then she thought of her egg, and flew down to the branches of a gum-tree to watch.

'The Great One trod on the egg, and broke the shell in two pieces, but he saw it not. As soon as the shell was broken, a black man came out of it, and stood behind him with a death-spear in one hand, a shield in the other, and red and yellow stripes on his face and breast, all ready to fight.

'"This is a strange place," said the Great One, looking at the mouthful of water he left in the water-hole. "Nothing stops the same. Up near the sun the stars keep on shining and do not change. The moons get big and small, but do not run away. But here everything is the same as a star with a tail and no head, that wanders about like dust, and goes out of sight like smoke. I did but turn my back and the egg is gone out of the water, the frog is not to be seen and the tadpole is standing upside down, with his tail as big as his head!"

'"Who gave you leave to count the things in my water-hole?" said the black man, standing where he could be seen. The Great One looked at him, then lifted up his hand, and the black man stood still and could not move hand or foot.

'"This creature has more danger in him than all the rest," said the Great One. "He has a death-spear, he is cunning, hunger comes upon him two and three times in a day. I must keep him from the lake, till I get grass-sticks to make a fire, and cook fish and eat, till the sun has to run over the ground again, to get back to the east in time to make it morning."

'The Great One knew that the black man would not stand still when he was left alone. So he put thunder on one side of him, and lightning on the other, and said: "Keep still, or the lightning will make you blind, and the thunder will strike you on the head."

'The Great One saw that his grass-sticks were not at the water-hole, so he turned to the scrub, and found a grass-tree, and broke it in the middle. But before he could finish making the two pieces, that kindle a fire when rubbed together, he heard a great noise. The reason was that the blue dove, who had seen the black man come out of her egg, had flown on the top of his head, so as to hatch him back into a proper creature.

'"Go away from the top of my head, you make me feel bad," said the black man.

'"Coo, coo, coo," said the dove, which meant, "No, no, no, you belong to me, I saw you come out of my egg, but the shell was broken before the time, so you came out wrong. Instead of being a big black thing with a beard and a death-spear, you ought to be a pretty little blue dove, that I could cover with my wings, that I could feed with a worm, and that would sleep all night against my heart."

'"Your claws are scratching the top of my head," said the black man, "and you make me feel bad. Thunder stands on one side of me, and lightning on the other. If I move, the thunder will strike me and the lightning make me blind. But that is better than having you hatch me. If you do not go away, I will strike you with my spear."

'"Coo, coo, coo," said the dove. "Every word you say shows that you have come out wrong. I must hatch you till you come out right, even if it takes a whole moon."

'The blue dove settled down faster than before on the head of the black man, and began to sing coo, coo, coo to herself in a low voice, so as to pass away the time. The black man raised his death-spear to strike her. The lightning flashed on one side of him, and the thunder crashed on the other. The blue dove flew to the top of the gum-tree, and the black man stood still where he was. The lightning passed out of sight, and left a little smell of burning, but blinded no one. The thunder struck no one, only left a sound that died away. The black man spoke no word, but closed his eyes, so as to make-believe he was blind.

'"How is it with you?" said the Great One, standing before him.

'The black man kept his eyes fast shut, and spoke no word.

'"Did I not tell you, that if you moved, evil would come to you?" said the Great One. "Yet you did not obey. Now behold – the thunder has made you dumb, and the lightning has made you blind."

'When he heard this, the black man opened his eyes wide, and laughed aloud.

'"You spoke of the lightning and of the thunder," he said, "but worse came to me of which you told me nothing. A bird came and made a nest of my head, to turn me into a creature with feathers and a beak. I called to her once, I called to her twice to go away. I spoke to her of thunder and of lightning, but she moved not – only spoke and tried to make me think that I had come out wrong, and must be hatched until I came out right. She fastened her claws into the top of my head and sang, coo, coo, coo, as if I were a foolish egg, in a nest of grass and broken sticks. Could any man that held a death-spear in his right hand, stand still and suffer that?"

'"It is the Blue Dove again," said the Great One, with the voice that was so big, it made the trees shake, now become a thin whisper.

'He threw down the grass-sticks that were not quite ready for use, he let his great basket fall, drew his cloak of red kangaroo skin round him and whispered low, "Each time that I have found a new world, the Blue Dove has come, and made all things go crooked." As the Great One spoke, he passed out of sight.

'When he was gone, the black man kindled a fire with the grass-sticks, cooked fish and ate, till the sun had to run over the earth again, to get back to the east in time to make the morning. The frog woke up and croaked for his mate; the old platypus let his wife come back to their mia-mia in the bank of the creek; the tadpole stood on his head and got fatter; the tiny fish in the swamp got a bigger tail, and the Blue Dove sang "Coo, coo, coo, coo," in the top of a tall gum-tree.'

'Is that the end?' asked Iliapa, who had listened to every word without closing an eye.

'Yes, that is all this time,' replied Polde. 'But the Great One and the Blue Dove often met, and every time they saw each other there was a story.'

Polde turned over and made her little blue blanket into a fresh shape under her head, and both were soon fast asleep.

This was the first day, and the first camp of the journey.

CHAPTER 11

On the second day they went on before the break of day, and walked some miles before the sun rose. By this time they had left the well-wooded country behind, and entered on a barren tract, where the only trees to be seen were those that lined the beds of creeks and shallow swamps, most of them now quite dry.

At mid-day they came to a wide watercourse, and followed it for half a mile, until they found a small pool of water. Here they made a quart-pot of tea, and ate the last of the mutton they brought with them and a couple of the big bush biscuits. After doing so, there were only three left. Polde looked at these half sadly and said, 'When we sit down to camp, I must look for something to kill.'

The sun was now so blazing hot, that the wind which was high, and blowing from the north-east, felt as if it came out of a furnace. So they lay down in the shade of a boxwood-tree, and rested and slept for some hours. When they arose, they were surprised to see how small the pool of water had become.

'We must always take care to keep some water in the bag,' said Iliapa, filling it, after they had each drunk a pannikinful. 'In a day or two we may have to camp where there is no water.'

Polde laughed, and said she was like the medicine man who turned into a hawk to get away from his enemies, and got so far off that there was nothing left but the sky and a few stars. It amused her when Iliapa looked ahead. It is not the way with Australian natives, who have lived from hand to mouth, from one generation to another, forced to let the morrow take care of itself. Polde, though she had lived so much with white people, never got out of this way, but Iliapa had learned to think of the future. She knew from her long journeys with her father that the early part of the day was always the best for travelling, and that therefore the night camp should be, if possible, by water, so as to make an early start without having to search for some. But as night fell, they looked in vain for this kind of camping-site.

They walked steadily on, cheered by the light of the moon, and of the stars that filled the sky. They stopped at several places, thinking, 'Surely there must be water here'; now in the bed of a creek, again where there was a dip in the country, or further on at traces of a shallow well. But the days of late had been terribly hot, the wind high and scorching, so that between them, they had dried up all the water that was merely on the surface.

'We have plenty in the bag for to-night; let us drink it, and go to sleep and look for more in the morning,' said Polde. And indeed they had travelled so many miles, and so many hours, that they were both dead tired. But Iliapa looked around in the moon- and star-light, and said she was sure they were getting near water. The way was now sandy, with low creeping bushes, and little or no grass. Away in the distance southward, there was a slight rise covered with trees; Polde looked long at these and then said:

'They are gum-trees; if it is the place I think, there is a little gorge in the range, with a water-hole that does not dry up.' So after resting for half an hour, and drinking some water, they went on to the range. It took them a long time to get there. The sand was now deep, and there were prickly bushes, and high tussocks of spinifex, which they had to avoid, so as not to get their legs and feet scratched and torn. Even a man with strong boots does not care to face spinifex. As it was, they got some scratches that drew blood. Iliapa said nothing of her mishaps, but Polde's laments were loud.

'There is a prickle in the big toe of my right foot, and the blood is running down my shins,' she said, half crying. 'It is horrid. We ought to have gone to sleep, when the sand began. Perhaps, after all, there is not a drop of water near that ugly range.'

'Oh yes, there is water and food, and see, there are some grass-trees,' replied Iliapa. 'When we get to the water, we will take one of the grass-trees and make such a fine fire for cooking.'

They had got to the foot of the range as she was speaking, and she hurried on ahead to the gap that seemed to hold the promise of water. It was only a steep little gully; there was no water.

'It is empty, it is empty,' cried Polde, who had pressed after her. Then she sat on the ground, and said it was no use going on in the night-time. Iliapa felt terribly cast down also, for the fear returned to her: 'What if the water is *all* dried up?' But she said nothing. She sat down and rested near Polde, and looked closely along the range, well-marked against the cloudless sky. As she looked, she saw there was a cleft that seemed to be about half a mile away.

'Perhaps that is the gully that has the pool of water,' she said to herself, her hopes rising once more.

'Polde, I believe I can see the gorge you meant,' she said. But Polde made no reply. She was lying down with one hand under her head, fast asleep. 'I will leave her here until I see whether I am right,' thought Iliapa. 'If not, then we must sleep until the day comes, and look for water in the daylight.'

So she stole quietly away, and walked very quickly to the cleft. As she drew near it, she thought at one moment that it must be the right gully; the next she was afraid it was not. But when she began to go down the side, she found the ground was covered with low bushes and green plants.

'Ah, there must be water,' she thought, 'nothing else would make the plants green.' As she went on, it seemed to her that she could smell a spring – there was a faint smell of moisture in the air. When she was near the bottom of the gully, she saw a sight that filled her with joy. There were the stars up in the sky, and stars down below.

'They are looking at themselves in the water, and it is beautiful,' she thought joyfully. And so it was. Clear, fresh, cold water, and plenty of it. She knelt down and drank of it as if she could not have enough. Then she filled the water-bag, and hurried back to Polde.

Polde was still fast asleep, and when Iliapa awoke her, she sat up and said in a grumbling tone, 'The water has all gone away from this ugly range. Now I am so thirsty, my tongue is dry and thick.'

'Well, there is still some water left in the bag,' said Iliapa; 'drink it up, I have had enough.'

Polde took the bag and drank greedily. 'It is quite cool and fresh, and the bag is full,' she said in a tone of wonder, after taking a deep draught. Iliapa laughed and told her what had happened.

'Let us camp up there, we may find something to eat,' said Polde, rising up quite briskly. And so they did. For after they got to the gorge and camped under a gum, they heard the hissing of a 'possum high in the tree. Looking up, they saw that where one of the thick branches had fallen off, there was a hollow place in the broken end. Polde at once knew what to do. She took the little sharp tomahawk, and making notches for her feet, as she went, climbed up the trunk until she got among the boughs. When there, she put a finger in her mouth, and made a strange low hissing, for all the world like a snake that is angry. Almost every creature is afraid of that sound.

After a short time a large 'possum came scurrying down from a topmost branch, and ran into the hollow at the end of the bough. This was what Polde had been playing for, and in a short time the 'possum was killed and roasting on a bright fire made of grass-tree.

One might think that after such a long fatiguing day, the two would go to sleep, as soon as eating had taken away the desire for food. But no, when they had eaten and rested, they were both so much awake that for a time they could not go to sleep, but sat and talked, while the grass-tree went on merrily burning, and giving out a fine aromatic scent, that was a little like almond blossom.

'You see what a good thing it is that I came with you. Always I can catch a big lizard, or kill a fat 'possum, or dig up a yelka, or snare a bird,' said Polde in a contented voice. 'It is good that the moon is with us, often you can catch things in the moonlight you cannot get near in the day. It would be fine if we could steal a moon like the 'Possum-man.'

'Who was the 'Possum-man and how could he steal a moon?'

'The 'Possum-man,' replied Polde, 'lived in the country of the Salt Water. One day when he was going to a creek to catch fish he saw a Kurdaitcha man – one who was going out alone to kill an enemy, and he had shoes of a very strange kind.'

'I know the sort of shoes,' said Iliapa. 'They are made of feathers and strong grass stuck together with blood and thin string. The heels and the toes are the same size, and the middle is no thicker than the ends; so they make no tracks that can be followed. But how did the 'Possum-man know, for the Kurdaitcha man would not wear them till he got near his enemy?'

'Because the kill-man had bands of charcoal on his body. When he saw this, the 'Possum-man was very much afraid, and he crept behind a low ti-tree bush, that grew thick on the banks of the creek, where he was going to get fish. "Here I will stay until the Kurdaitcha man goes on his way," he said. While he waited he fell asleep. When he woke up the sun had gone back into the earth. He was hungry and it was too late to catch fish. The Kurdaitcha man had gone, but another had come, and made a fire, and put boughs around it on the banks of the creek, near the ti-tree where the 'Possum-man slept. He was an old man with a white beard. He sat by the fire, and the air was full of the smell of cooking. The 'Possum-man drew up the air into his nostrils, and his bowels were sore with hunger.

'"The old man is cooking fish and a duck. I will go down and sit a little way from him. If he does not call me to come, and offer me some food, then I must take some as if it were my own. He is an old man, and I am young. His back is bent, and mine is straight."

'So the 'Possum-man took up his spear and shield, his netted bag, and the long stick with the noose at the end of it, with which he was going to catch fish. He went close up to where the old man could see him. He stuck his spear into the ground, and sat down. But the old man was eating as fast as a hawk flies after a little bird, and never looked up nor down, nor round about him. The 'Possum-man coughed out loud. But the old man had taken the duck from under the earth and the heated stones, and in one mouthful all the breast disappeared; in another the wings and a leg. Then the 'Possum-man saw that the old man had a great mouth from ear to ear, and rising up quickly, he ran to him, crying: "All day long have I eaten nothing, and hunger is tearing me like the hind claws of an old man kangaroo."

'"How sorry I am," said the old man, "for this is all that is left." He held up a handful of fish bones, and the head and the two claws of the duck; the 'Possum-man sat down by the fire and groaned out loud. For great hunger was with him, making all his body to ache as if with the bite of an evil cat. Now the Ungamilla – the evening star – was in the sky and how should he fish or catch bird or beast?

'"The fish in this creek are many and good to eat," said the old man. "But the night has now come, when you cannot see to catch them. So I will give you a light that will not go out. When you have caught as many fish as you can eat, bring it back to me. Here it is." He went behind the ti-tree bushes, and brought back his shield. On the shield there was the moon – large, round and white – giving so much light that it made the night like day. The 'Possum-man took the shield with the moon on it, and in a little time he caught more fish than he could eat.

'Then he thought: "It is a very good thing to have a moon that you can carry about. . . . I will . . . not give . . . ba-ac-k."' The last few words were very slowly spoken. There was silence for a little. Then Polde went on in her broken English, speaking in a dream-like tone: "And so the bestest lille Queen of Inglan' an' of the Blacks she stuck her dimeng crown on a gol' plate. . . . "

'Polde, what in the world are you saying?' cried Iliapa in a laughing voice. The only reply was a gentle snore. Polde, in falling asleep, had gone back to tales well known to her, when she was so much with the Moorano children. Iliapa looking up into the sky, full of stars, thought of Alibaka and his father. 'Would they ever see each other again? Yes, yes,' she said, half-aloud, as if to keep her fears at a distance. 'Even now Nalbuka may be on his way from the country to the Great Salt Water.'

CHAPTER 12

They awoke next morning before the sun had risen. When it first came in sight, it looked like a great red angry ball of fire, and already the wind, blowing from the north-east, was quite warm.

'It is going to be a very hot day,' said Iliapa. 'Let us get on as fast as we can, for we must stop when the sun gets high.'

Polde, who was still lying down, stretched out her arms and gave a big yawn. Then she looked at the red sun, and said in a sleepy voice, 'The water here is so good – what if we stop till the sun gets low?'

But by this time Iliapa was going down to the water-hole, where she drank a long deep draught, and then filled the bag. As she was coming back, she heard Polde's voice shrill with delight.

'Two great big ones, here they were quite near me, covered over with sand. Oh, what a fine thing for us, and there is the stump of the grass-tree still burning. We can cook them at once.'

It was two large emu eggs that she had found, where some mother emu had covered them over, and left them to be hatched by the sun. They cooked and ate them – one each, and went on their way a little after the sun rose.

After a few miles, the country opened out into a plain, marked here and there by creeks, lined with gum- and box-trees. That is the beds of creeks, for there was now no sign of water in them.

At mid-day they halted by a native well, in a gully full of trees, close to a wide watercourse of glittering sand. There was not much in the well, but when they dug a little the water rose slowly. They found a good many yams, and some big grubs in the gum-trees. After eating these with the last biscuits, they went to sleep in the shade of the trees for two hours. On awaking they made a quart-pot of tea, which greatly refreshed them.

When they went on their way again, the wind had changed, and was blowing high from the north. It was at their backs, and helped them on. The sun, too, became overcast with clouds, so that it was not as hot as the day before.

'You thought we should get to Ekunja Hill a little after the sun goes down,' said Iliapa, as they rested an hour before sunset, on the top of a low rise covered with salt-bush and tufts of coarse high grass, that the sun had bleached quite white and dry. Polde was so busy looking for something to eat that she made no reply. In a few minutes she came upon a large iguana lizard, and after killing it, went on with her search. 'For that thing is not more than enough for Iliapa, and I can always eat more than she does,' she thought to herself. She was still searching in vain for something more to eat, when she heard Iliapa calling her.

'See what I have found here, pushed away under this salt-bush,' she said, when Polde came up to her. It was a wallet or sort of native portmanteau, made of wallaby skin, with the fur left on, very much like the one that Yukuta had when he went to the corroboree at Okalparra. Iliapa and Polde had often seen one of them, but never the things they held, any more than they had seen the tribal ceremonies, in which only the men take part. So they were greatly excited and interested, and Iliapa was even a little afraid, as they opened out the wallet, and looked at the things that were in it, one by one.

These are most of them: Tufts of eagle hawk feathers; two long bunches of emu feathers; a bunch of the long tail-feathers of the black cockatoo; a lump of porcupine grass resin; two pieces of red ochre; one of yellow, and two of white pipe-clay; a large tuft of the tail tips of the rabbit-kangaroo; the dried crop of an eagle filled with down; two pieces of flint. There was also a piece of wad, which when rubbed up, makes a bluish grey powder, that black men rub on their bodies, for some of their ceremonies by way of decoration. The thing that made Iliapa rather afraid, was a long waist-girdle of human hair.

'It is forbidden (ekirnija),' she said, hiding it under the bush.

'I wish we could take them all with us,' said Polde, looking from one object to the other with longing eyes. There was a ball of opossum fur string that both felt was too useful to be left.

'The red ochre too, and the tail tips of the rabbit-kangaroo we must take,' said Iliapa.

'But these are not nearly as pretty as the tufts of feathers and the white down,' replied Polde.

'But don't you know how good red ochre is if you get ill, and the tail tips if some night we want to keep awake,' said Iliapa.

So in the end these were the only three things they took. The rest they put back in the wallet and placed it where they found it, under the salt-bush.

Finding this treasure delayed them, so that the sun had gone down when Ekunja Hill came in sight. At the foot of this hill, where two creeks met, there was a deep water-hole, that was famous for never getting dry, even in the hottest summers. For this reason there are generally in such seasons many water-fowl here, that gather in from the dry regions, and naked deserts near and far.

'Don't make a noise or speak loud,' said Polde in a whisper, when she saw that round most of the water-hole, reeds and bulrushes were growing thick and high. Then she stole round to the eastern end while Iliapa gathered sticks to make a fire. In less than twenty minutes Iliapa heard the frightened squeak of a bird, while a flock rose into the air, and many plunged into the water. Polde had caught a large duck among the reeds, and when they had cooked and eaten it, Iliapa said they could keep the iguana lizard for the morning. But Polde said she would get something else for the next day, and having cooked it, she picked the white flesh off the lizard, and ate it, down to the last joint of its backbone.

'Now you will not want anything to eat till we stop to-morrow at mid-day. We must start away from here before the sun rises, for you said there are rocks and much sand between this and the next water,' said Iliapa, who was vexed to see the big lizard eaten, when it would save time to have it in the morning.

'You do not think of anything but getting away early and walking late,' replied Polde crossly. 'When we come to a good water-hole like this, with fine fat ducks, we ought to stop a little time.'

'If we stop and eat all the fat ducks, I shall never get to my boy at all,' answered Iliapa.

'Yai, yai, Malarai . . .' began Polde in a mocking voice. But all at once she stopped, while Iliapa sprang to her feet. What was that they heard in the distance? They both listened without drawing a breath. Yes, it was the queer, half-muffled bark of a half-bred native dog. It is only the blacks who have such dogs. There must be some of them coming to this water-hole.

The thought filled both of them with terror. Iliapa, without a moment's pause, began to gather up their few belongings. Polde still listened, hoping it might turn out to be some lost dog, that was straying in the wilds without a master. But after a minute or two, she heard a voice crying out in the Arunta tongue. 'Come on, come on, the water-hole is near.' Iliapa heard also, and stood for a little, cold with fear. It seemed to her that it was the voice of Yukuta.

'If it is the men of the Ring-necked Parrot, they will knock me on the head, because Loatjira killed one of their boys; if they are men of the Plum-tree they will take me away, because my cousin stole one of their girls,' said Polde, who was so much alarmed that she spoke in a hoarse whisper.

'If it is Yukuta – and he sees me, he will know I am going for my boy,' said Iliapa slowly.

'Yukuta,' repeated Polde is a frightened voice. 'Has he found out you are on the way to Labalama? Oh, we shall both be killed like wombats in a hole,' she cried, letting the things she had been gathering drop from her hands.

'No, no, no,' cried Iliapa, with sudden energy, gathering them up in haste. 'Don't you see they are on the other side of the water-hole; they will stop there and drink water and rest; they will not move further till the morning. Come away, come away – we shall get far this very night. To-morrow we shall cross the rocky hills. After that you said the way is good till we come to the Red Sand Desert.'

While Iliapa was talking, she had finished putting their things together, and then turned to help Polde, who was in such a tremor that she hardly knew what she was doing.

'Why are you taking that?' asked Iliapa, pointing to a crooked, useless stick in Polde's netted bag. She had put it there instead of the strong well-fashioned stick, sharp at one end and thick at the other, which she used for digging up yams and killing small game. Iliapa could not help laughing when she saw the foolish thing that had been so carefully put in the bag, while the good stick was left lying on the ground. Then Polde took courage and began to feel better.

They stole away in the twilight, round by the end of the water-hole that was furthest from the side on which the strange blacks had camped.

'See, they have made two fires – there must be men and women,' said Polde, standing to look back, from the side of the Ekunja Hill above the water-hole. 'What a sad thing to leave all those fine ducks,' she added to herself in a lower tone. But Iliapa hurried her on, and soon they had crossed the gravelly channel of one of the creeks, as they struck out southward from Ekunja Hill.

The way lay over ground that now and then rose in stony ridges, which made it hard travelling for naked feet. But when the light of the stars was added to that young moon, they could pick their steps better, and get on faster.

After some hours, they stopped at a wide water-course, and found a sheltered place in which to sleep. They were going to drink out of the water-bag, when Iliapa noticed a spot that looked damp. She scooped up the ground and then dug it, with the sharp end of Polde's stick. Some coloured water rose slowly. It was a little salt, but Iliapa found it good enough to drink. She always liked to keep the bag full, for fear of having to stop where no water could be found.

'For we might go round and round, and find no water, until we had to lie down and die. Then what would come of Alibaka.' Alibaka, Alibaka, – that was the beginning and the end of all her thoughts.

'What if he should not be in Labalama at all, when I get there,' she said to herself, half aloud, after lying down to sleep.

'What is that you are saying about a fat duck?' asked Polde in a sleepy voice.

'Yai, yai, Malarai,' replied Iliapa, imitating Polde's way of repeating these words, when anything was said to which she did not want to give a straight answer.

In a few minutes both were fast asleep.

CHAPTER 13

Wake up, Polde; the sun is getting old in the sky,' said Iliapa when she opened her eyes next morning to find her companion still fast asleep. Polde rubbed her eyes, and turned over on the other side.

'Last night we walked till after midnight, I must sleep a little longer,' she said, settling herself comfortably in the shade of the group of desert oaks under which they had camped. Seeing that she was so tired, Iliapa left her, and began to look round for something to eat before they went on their way.

But the country was very bare. They had now come on the borders of a tract of stony land, with rocky hills, no creeks, and only a few desert oaks, and stunted bushes here and there. She saw some pigeons flying overhead, and in the distance she saw what looked to her like a kangaroo. But such game was beyond their powers of killing or catching, and Iliapa would have been very glad if she could find even a big lizard or a little snake – anything, in fact, that had flesh on its bones.

She walked to the top of one of the stony hills, looking very closely on the ground as she went. But she saw nothing that had the breath of life in it – only withered grass, low bushes, and stones that lay so loose, they rolled down the hillside when her feet touched them.

'I am not a good hunter, but even Polde could hardly find anything here,' she thought as she stood on the hill and looked around.

There was a rough bush track running between the hills from east to west. As Iliapa stood there, thinking how hard it would be to get across this piece of country, without any food, she saw a little cloud of dust arising on the road westward.

Watching this, she soon saw that it was a light American wagon drawn by two horses, and that there were two persons in the trap.

The track wound round the foot of the hill, on which she stood, and as the wagon came nearer, Iliapa saw that the two persons in it were a man and a woman. This made her feel very happy, for white women had always been kind to her. She had the feeling that this one, too, would somehow be able to help them.

So she went quickly down the hillside, and stood close to the track, waiting for the wagon. As it drove near, the people looked hard at her, and at first Iliapa thought they were going to drive on. But the woman said something Iliapa could not hear, and the man drew in the horses.

'Good morning,' said Iliapa, in such good English that the two in the buggy were much surprised.

'Are you here all alone?' asked the white woman.

'No, my mate is asleep; her name is Polde, and I have come to look for something to eat,' replied Iliapa. The white woman asked her how they came to be alone, without any man to hunt for them. On this Iliapa told her story. When the white woman heard how Yukuta had sold the poor mother's only child and how the boy had been taken away by a white man, she seemed as if she could hardly believe her ears.

But her husband, who was listening to all that had been said, now spoke out in a loud angry voice:

'Yes, it is that rascal Simon – it is just like him. He passed through some days ago, on his way to Labalama with some horses he bought at one of the stations. I saw him and a black boy riding with him. If I had only known how the scoundrel came by the lad!'

'You saw Alibaka – you saw my boy!' cried Iliapa.

All at once she began to cry. Yet it was not sorrow that made her tears fall so fast. It was a kind of joyous relief to be at last quite sure that her boy had been taken to Labalama, and that she would find him there.

'My poor, poor girl – how will you ever get there through such desert country? And in the summer too, when the days are often frightfully hot,' said the white woman, who on seeing Iliapa cry for her lost boy, could not keep back her own tears. But Iliapa soon dried her eyes.

'I can get there all right, my mate is a fine hunter,' she said. 'After we pass through this stony country, the Red Sand Desert is not so very far away. Then we go with the iron poles that carry news for you, and find creeks and wells and dams all the way to Labalama.'

'But you were looking for something to eat, and have found nothing,' said the white woman. 'Oh, how glad I am that you waited for us here, for we can give you plenty to help you over this stony place where you can find so little.'

She and her husband got out of the wagon, and letting down the backboard, opened a bag in which there was some mutton. They were people who had a small sheep run, and they were going with some rations to two men who were sinking a well some miles beyond the hill at which Iliapa met them.

They gave her a good large piece of meat, many pounds of flour, with a little packet of salt and some tea and sugar. For they knew that natives who have got used to the food of white people get very fond of tea.

'You have had nothing to eat this morning and it will take some time to make a damper,' said the white woman; 'take this for your breakfast,' and she cut a large loaf of bread in two, and put half into a little bag with the rest of the food; also half a dozen of the square thick bush biscuits. The husband would have added a box of matches, but Iliapa told him that they had enough for the whole journey.

'Good-bye and the best of luck to you,' they said as they were getting into the wagon. And the husband added as they were driving away, 'If you were going our way I would give you a lift. I'll write to some one at Labalama, who will help to get your boy from that rascal who stole him away from you.'

Iliapa could not find words with which to thank them for all their kindness. She was as happy as a bird on the wing, and indeed almost went as fast, all the way back to the group of desert oaks, under which she had left Polde lying.

She was still fast asleep, and Iliapa gathered sticks and made a fire, without saying a word to waken her. She filled the quart pot with water – not from the bag, but from the hole scooped in the bed of the creek, in which more water had risen during the night. When the water boiled, she put a big handful of tea and sugar into it, having still more than half of what they had taken with them.

Then she cut off a good large piece of the mutton, and put it on the fire, which had burned down to a steady glow.

'When it is cooked,' she thought, 'I will call Polde. She will think it is like a tale from the long-ago (Alcheringa) when she sees all the food that I have got.' But before the mutton was quite cooked, Polde moved in her sleep, and began to murmur something about 'a fat duck.' On hearing this, Iliapa burst into a hearty laugh. Polde, who was just waking up after her long sleep, turned round, and putting her elbow on the ground, rested her head on her hand, and looked at Iliapa with a face full of wonder. There were some bushes between, so she could not see what was on the fire. But there was a delicious smell of cooking in the air, which Polde sniffed once and again.

'Who was that laughing,' she asked, 'or was it part of my dream? and is this nice smell awake, or will it go away when I get up? . . . Oh, how hungry I am, and what can I get among these stones? . . . It is no use asking you to hunt for anything – you never can get even a bat. But this fine smell seems to be quite awake. Tell me, Iliapa, have you got a bird or a fish, or something really nice?'

Polde got up as she was speaking, and came to the fire. There was a great piece of fine white bread and six big biscuits on the top of the little bag; there was a quart-pot full of tea by the fire; and there was a great piece of mutton frizzling on the coals.

Polde looked from one thing to the other, and then at Iliapa, in a kind of stupor.

'Go and lie down, Polde, for you are full of sleep and dreams,' said Iliapa slyly. 'If you lie down you will eat all these things that you see. Think what a nice dream that will be.'

Without saying a word, Polde took the pannikin, and filled it with tea out of the quart pot. She broke the half loaf of bread in two, got the sharp clasp-knife, and cut some ribs from the mutton that was frizzling on the coals. Still without saying a word, she began to eat and to drink.

Iliapa sat down near her and did the same. After a little time, Polde took breath to say: 'Did you ever in all your life eat anything that had such a nice taste as this mutton? And tea in the morning – we never had that before on this journey.'

'Was it not a good thing that I went out to look for food this morning?' rejoined Iliapa, laughing.

'Never again will I say that you are not a good hunter,' replied Polde with great fervour. When at last she had finished eating, she begged to know how it all happened. When she heard that the white man had really seen Alibaka with the one who stole him, on their way to Labalama, she gave a little shout of joy.

'Did I not tell you,' she said, 'that you will be finding him there all safe and well? Ah, what a fine day that will be for us when you see one, two, three, and one, two, three smokes going up into the sky, and say, "What is it making all these smokes?" Then I climb a gum-tree like an opossum and look all round, from the east to the west and from the north to the south. And there in the south, what do I see? The houses of Labalama, the long carts on wheels, with a fire at one end, and no horses, going like the wind to the far-away big Adelaide.'

Iliapa listened as if she had never heard before of this happy day to come. The thought made her laugh with pleasure. But she soon became very grave, thinking of the long hard way that they must travel before she could get to her boy. She rose up quickly to make ready for a start. 'Labalama is still nearly a moon away,' she said, 'and we have this stony country to get over, and the desert to cross before we come to the land of many waters. We are late to-day – it is time we begun to walk.'

'If we stay a little longer, we need not stop any more till the moon and stars come out. See what a nice fire is here; let us cook the rest of the meat, to keep it from going bad, and to have it ready,' said Polde, who did not feel at all tempted to begin to walk hard as soon as she had finished swallowing a big meal. Iliapa knew that the mutton would keep better when it was cooked. So they cut it in two pieces, roasted them, and at last got away when the sun was high in the sky. But it was covered with clouds, and the wind had again risen, and was blowing from the north.

'Fine wind that you are to help us on the way; fine wind that you are to help us on the way,' crooned Polde, as they started, each feeling strong and well and in good spirits.

They crossed many rocky hills, and many stony gullies, stopping now and then for a little rest, and when they got very tired. Then on again, up and down; across gullies, and up and down hills.

An hour before sunset they came on a native well in the bottom of a gully. There was a little sweet water in it. They filled the water-bag and made tea; drank a pannikinful turn about, and munched one of the big bush biscuits. Then once more, up and down rocky hills, and across stony gullies, until at sunset, they thought they were near the end of this hard, bare land of stone and hill. They reached a narrow but well-wooded valley, with a bank of whitish clay, crossing it like a wall. Beyond this there was one rocky hill, and further on a dim reddish-looking plain.

'That is the Red Sand Desert,' said Iliapa. 'To-night we shall camp in this valley of trees.'

CHAPTER 14

It was hardly daylight when Iliapa was awakened by some curious noise close to her head. It was a bird with a whistling note, in the branches of the box-tree under which they had slept. Her legs and back ached all over, with yesterday's rough travelling up and down so many hills and over so many stones.

But when she moved about, getting wood to make a fire, she felt better. When the water boiled, she made the tea, and called Polde, who got up without one word of grumbling.

'It is a fine thing to sit down and eat, without having to go hunting in the trees or over the ground,' she said cheerfully, as she began to eat bread and mutton and drink tea. They could see it was going to be a very hot day again, so they ate a good deal of the meat, and kept the five big biscuits for their evening meal. They got away at sunrise, and twenty minutes later they got to the top of that last rocky hill.

It was not quite the same as most of the other hills they had passed. The rocks were larger, and there were bigger crevices between them. Polde cried out that she saw something move in one of these openings.

'Perhaps it is a fine fat wombat,' she said, as she spoke removing a large stone.

'But even if it is, we cannot wait now to hunt and kill it,' replied Iliapa. 'We have enough food for nearly three days, and we must not load ourselves up with more, going through the Red Sand Desert.'

Polde made no answer. She stood at the opening below the big stone she had moved, like one made stupid by a knock on the head.

'Oh, Iliapa,' she at last exclaimed, 'come here – come and look at this.'

Iliapa ran up at once, and looked in. It was a curious sight that she saw. A little stone cave, with walls rubbed fine and smooth, and all over them the strange things drawn that were never seen on sea or land.

Eight- and ten-footed creatures, with great horns and long bushy tails, and eyes large, round and red as the coals of a mallee-root fire. Immense coiling serpents, with long stings thrust out of the mouth, as if ready to fly at and sting the beholder to death on the spot. Other queer signs and symbols that it would be hard to describe. Then a cloud of birds with outspread wings. They were all drawn solid in charcoal, with a line of red ochre running round them. As soon as Iliapa saw the birds, she cried out:

'This is the Ernatulunga – (the sacred storehouse) – of the Rock-Pigeon Men. Come away, Polde. See these bundles on the floor. . . . They are the Churinga of the spirit people.'

But Polde laughed, and said she was not afraid of the spirits or the bodies of the Rock-Pigeon Men; she did not care a feather for the Churinga or the Long-Ago. She took up one of the bundles that lay on the floor. It was carefully wrapped round in a small rug made of wild-cat skins, and tied with kangaroo tendons. The moment Polde touched this bundle, Iliapa gave a cry of fear, and covered her face with her hands. When after a second or two she looked up, and saw that Polde was really opening the bundle, she turned and fled, crying, 'For your life, don't look or touch.'

She had not gone far when she heard Polde give a shriek of fear, and come hurrying after her.

'What is it? What did you see?' asked Iliapa, greatly moved. Polde's eyes were wide open with terror, and the sweat was pouring down her face.

'Something moved in a dark corner,' she said brokenly when she was a little calmer. 'Something big . . . that made a strange noise . . . with eyes that flared at me.'

'I told you not to look or touch,' said Iliapa. 'Let us get away as fast as we can; something awful might happen to us, after doing such a trick. Do you not know that with the Aruntas, no women or boys are ever allowed to look on the things that belong to the spirit people? If the Rock-Pigeon Men found us here, or knew that one of us touched the Churinga, they would kill us on the spot, or else put out our eyes with a fire-stick.'

'The wicked dogs, I would put out their eyes with my digging-stick,' cried Polde, almost as angry as if she saw a Rock-Pigeon Man coming after her with a blazing fire-stick.

'No, no, Polde – you would run away as fast as your legs could carry you – but that would do no good, for the Rock-Pigeon Men are strong and cunning. Oh, come away.' Iliapa, who had gathered up all the things she carried, now began to go down the hill. 'I shake with fear when I think what there may be in that cave. . . . Will it perhaps follow us?'

'Very likely it was a wombat after all – or perhaps a great snake, that has got fat and old, eating creatures that creep into the cave at night. . . . Things often look strange in the dark,' replied Polde. She had got over the worst of her fright, and began to think that, after all, there could be nothing so very dreadful in that little cave with the strange drawings on the walls.

She had not been brought up to believe in the things that Iliapa had been taught. That was why she made light of the sacred storehouse of the Arunta, and the objects that they hold in such awe. Still she kept very close to Iliapa, as they went quickly down the other side of that rocky hill, and now and then she cast a hasty glance behind, as if to make sure that no fearful creature was on their track.

It was close on mid-day when they came to the edge of the real desert of sand. Here there was a dip in the country, and the wide shallow bed of a creek, lined with low bushes, and straggling gum-trees that gave little shade.

Going on westward, they found the creek bed getting deeper and wider, with several holes that had been scooped out for water.

'These holes were made not long ago,' said Iliapa, as they stood by one in a sandy hollow, 'and they were made by black men, for see here the tracks of naked feet.'

'And here is a broken digging-stick,' said Polde, going on a little further. This broken stick was close to a hole that was deeper than the rest. There was a little water at the bottom of this, and although it was not very clear, it was sweet and fresh.

Here they halted before they began to cross the Red Sand Desert. To-day there was no wind at all, not one cloud in the sky, and the sun was blazing hot. They scooped out the hole that had water in it, to make it a little deeper. When they saw the water slowly rising, they used what they had in the bag, to make some tea, and in mixing some of the flour, that had been given them the day before.

Polde would have merely made up the flour with water and some salt into a thin dough, and then put it on the coals in handfuls so that it would have been burned on the outside and raw in the middle. But Iliapa said that this would waste the flour, and that she knew how to make a fine damper.

First she built a good fire of thickish sticks, in the bed of the creek. Then she put a third part of the flour on the outside of the bag in which it was carried, sprinkled some salt into it, and mixed it up by degrees with water, not too much at a time, until she made up the whole into a good stiff dough, that she kneaded up well and firmly. Then she spread it out into a good-sized round cake of equal thickness and made a little hole in the middle.

By this time the fire had burned down into a mass of glowing coals. Iliapa took the broken digging-stick they had found, and carefully cleared all the coals to one side, leaving only a thin coating of hot ashes on the ground. On this she placed the damper, and getting a piece of bark, she spread on the damper a coating of fine hot ashes. Over this she placed the coals, raising them in a mound, so that they would keep alight for some time.

While the damper was cooking, they lay down and slept in the shade on the bank of the creek. When they awoke, the sun was slanting westward, and all the coals over the damper had burned down into white hot ashes. When these were raked away, there it lay quite cooked, with a golden brown crust, that made Polde's mouth water.

'This is for the desert, when the sand makes us so tired, that we can hardly drag one leg after the other,' said Iliapa, 'and where there is hardly a stick or a bit of bark to be found to make a fire.'

'If the Rock-Pigeon Men came down on us, and killed us on the spot, because we went into their Churinga cave, they would take this fine damper away, and we would not know even the taste of it,' said Polde sadly.

'Well then, let us have a piece each while it is hot,' replied Iliapa, who found the smell of the fresh-baked bread so good that she was glad to eat some. Then they filled the water-bag as full as it would go, and went on their way.

Though the sun had lost some of its heat, and there was now a wind blowing from the north-east, the sand still felt very hot under their naked feet. It was heavy walking, for there was hardly any grass or plants to bind the sand, so that at every step it shifted under them. But they took long strides, and went on mile after mile without once stopping or saying a word.

Before sunset the sand became a little firmer, and there were groups of mulga- and box-trees here and there. Now walking was easier and they went on a good deal faster. The moon was now late in rising, but the stars were out all over the sky, giving a beautiful soft light. The sand had got much heavier again, and there were hardly any trees to be seen. There was no sign of water anywhere. They camped under a solitary tree and were so tired that they did not say a single word. The moment they lay down they were both fast asleep.

CHAPTER 15

It was a strange world on which they opened their eyes at daylight. The dawn was breaking and the whole of the east, right up to the centre of the sky, was a deep crimson. The sand that stretched around on every side, with hardly a rise or a hollow in its level expanse, caught a more sombre tinge of red from the deep colour above. Over all hung a haze of bluish smoke that made earth and sky look as if a sullen fire lay in smother, which would soon burst into flames that would sweep everything before them into ashes – where there was anything to burn. Here there was nothing but sand, in which no blade ever took root, where no bird ever built a nest, nor even a spider spun its web.

'There must be a fire not far away.' Iliapa as she spoke looked round in a half-dazed way. She had never before seen country that had only sand underfoot, a flaming sky overhead and smoke all round.

'They are burning spinifex away to the west,' said Polde. 'Once when I was in the Desert and the spinifex was on fire, the wind was blowing so high from the west – the smoke got into our eyes and noses, so that we cried like white babies. It is good the wind is from the north to-day – it will help us on the way.'

'Yes, and it is good you brought this bundle of sticks to make tea, and that we have such a nice damper.'

They tried to be cheerful and keep up their courage. But the sun, rushing up like a monstrous globe of fire, the wind getting higher and blowing as if from a furnace across endless leagues of sand, without shade or water, caused a sort of fear they could feel but not put into words. It was as though they had come to the end of all the pleasant visions of earth, and were facing a region of immeasurable thirst, on a day when the sun fastens on the earth like a fire, which eats out the heart of everything that has the sap of life.

Yet even at the worst the barest deserts are not in all places equally lacking in shelter: – an hour before mid-day they reached a wide watercourse with shelving banks, that gave them a refuge from the sun. The heat, the wind and the sand had made them so tired that they ate nothing before they lay down. They just drank a little water, and in a few minutes they were fast asleep.

When they awoke the sun was slanting westward; clouds had gathered in the sky, the wind had shifted to the east, and was not quite so high. It was with some trouble that they found enough fuel to boil water for tea. They walked along the banks of the watercourse until they came to the remains of some bushes. They were quite withered and as dry as tinder. They broke at a touch, and Iliapa went back with a bundle of them to their camping-place.

'I go a bit further,' said Polde, 'I think there is a stay-all-time water-hole near this.' In a short time she came to a deep hollow in this bed of the watercourse. At the bottom of this, the earth looked damp, which showed that there had been water lately, and that some might still be got by digging. This made Polde feel glad, for she could not bear to take small sips of water, when she wanted to drink two pannikinsful, one after the other.

She had her digging-stick with her, and scooped away at the damp spot, until she saw a little water slowly oozing up. She was hurrying back to tell Iliapa the good news, when she noticed some decayed leaves on the margin of the hollow. She saw that they were the leaves of flag-reeds, and at once dug for the roots, which when roasted are almost as nice to eat as potatoes. In a short time she got more than a dozen roots, and took back with her another bundle of withered shrub sticks, with which to roast some of them.

'What has been keeping you?' called Iliapa, as soon as Polde came in sight. 'You had better be quick or I shall drink up all the tea – I am so thirsty.'

'Well, drink it all up, and I will make another quart-potful for myself,' returned Polde, proud of having struck water, also of finding roots, where they never expected anything to eat.

When the roots were well roasted they both enjoyed them even more than the damper. The roots of the flag-reed are much better than yams; white people look upon them as the best vegetable food that can be found in the Bush.

Confident that they could fill the bag at the hole Polde had dug, they each drank as much tea and water as they wished for. But when they went to fill the bag, a mischance awaited them. The water was very brackish. It was not quite undrinkable, but it lacked the stimulating quality of fresh water.

'Polde, why did you not taste it?' cried Iliapa, rather mournfully. They had little more than a pannikinful left in the water-bag, and they were not quite half-way through the Red Sand Desert.

'We had better finish up the water in the bag and then fill it from the salty pool and walk as far as we can. When we are very thirsty and tired, the salty water will taste much better,' said Polde, true to her practice of never making a sacrifice of the present to the future hour. With a little hesitation, Iliapa assented. It might be better to mix the good water with the brackish. But the thirst of the desert was strong on both, and when they had divided the contents of the bag between them they filled it from the pool and went steadily on. Near sunset a low rise with a few straggling trees growing on it came in sight.

'We are well past the middle of the Desert now,' said Polde. 'There is a native well not far from these trees. We had better look for it in the morning and camp here to-night.'

But Iliapa thought they had better push on till they reached the trees.

Polde gave a low groan in reply. Walking so long and so hard through heavy sand, made her ache all over so much, that she felt ready to cry. But she did not give way.

'Iliapa must feel just as bad, and she says not a word,' she thought, hitching up the bundle on her back, so as to change the pressure on her shoulders, and making a great effort to walk a little faster. She could not, however, keep up with Iliapa, who, by degrees, came to be a couple of hundred yards ahead.

But when she was within a few minutes' walk of the first group of trees, all at once she stood quite still. Polde watched her, wondering what made her stand so very quiet, and looking all the time in front of her, as if she saw something queer or dreadful.

'What is it?' she asked, in a small tired voice, when she came within speaking distance.

'At first I could not be sure – it might be a little dust rising up into the air – but see now – it is getting bigger and it is blue, curling up above that patch of scrub, a little beyond the trees. It is the smoke of a camp!'

'It must be black people who know of the stay-all-time well – if it is a camp?'

There could be no doubt of it, for now the smoke rose thick and dark, as if fresh wood had been put on the fire.

'Yes, they must be blacks, by that fire – and who are they?' said Iliapa, speaking in a whisper, as though afraid of being heard all that way.

Before either of them could say another word, they heard a voice quite close to them saying in the Arunta tongue: 'Are you alone?' It was a black women who was all but naked. She had been crouching behind a ridge of sand, where she had hidden herself, when she first saw Iliapa and Polde, waiting to see what they were going to do. When she saw them staring at the fire-smoke, as if afraid to go on, she spoke.

'Yes, we are all alone,' replied Iliapa. 'Is that your camp where we see the smoke?'

'Yes, that is my camp,' answered the woman slowly, drawing nearer. 'My name is Wonka. There are three of us. My mother, who is very old, and Okula, who has a little baby. We belong to the Rock-Pigeon Men. We are going to Ekunja Hill, but when we came to the Imanka Well, my mother was so bad – every night she shook like a leaf when the wind was high. Okula had her baby, and my head was so bad, that when I looked at the earth, everything went round and round.

'That is what my head is doing now,' said Polde, pressing her two hands against her temples.

By this time they were all sitting down in the sand, and the sun had gone down, leaving all the sky high up in the west as red as if it had caught fire.

'Have you plenty water in the Imanka Well?' asked Iliapa.

'Yes, water so deep that you cannot get to the bottom,' replied Wonka.

On hearing this Iliapa handed the water-bag to Polde, saying, 'Drink – if you can – your head is going round, because you are so tired and so thirsty.'

Polde, without another word, took the bag and drained nearly a pannikinful without a shudder.

'Then you stayed behind while the men went on?' said Iliapa.

'Yes, the men sat in their camp and talked together,' replied Wonka. 'Next morning they went back to the water-hole we left behind, before we came to the Red Sand Desert. They got back after the sun had gone down. They had killed a small emu, and some other birds.

'They said, a message-stick has been sent to us – we must meet some of the Rock-Pigeon Men at the Ekunja Hill before the moon is two nights older. You cannot travel across the Red Sand Desert. One of you is too old, another is too ill, and the youngest has a small baby. So we leave you here with food, where there is plenty of water. In one, two, three, and one, two days, we shall come back. So they went away one, two days ago.

'My mother is very old. She cannot see till the sun is high in the sky. She can only hear when there is thunder in the clouds. We give her the flesh of the young emu, and she pushes it from her. We roast her a duck or a 'possum, but she throws it away. "Give me yelka," she says, and then she cries like a small child. I take my digging-stick; I come to search for yelka, or any root. I look across the sand to see if anything grows there. I see no green leaf, but there are two girls with things on their heads, with dresses on their bodies, like white women.

'Then I said, "Are there men coming with them, who will take away our food, who will beat us to death, because they are at war with the Rock-Pigeon Men?" Then I spoke. You say you are alone. Come with me then. Drink of our water, and eat of our food.'

'We will drink of your water, out of the Imanka Well, but food we have with us,' said Iliapa.

'And roots also,' added Polde, 'the roots of the flag-reed. They will make the inside of your mother to shiver with gladness.'

'What a fine thing it is,' she thought to herself, 'that we did not eat up all the roots. There are many left. When we give these to the old mother, they will surely give us a piece of emu flesh, of duck or 'possum.'

And that was indeed what took place. The old grandmother, whose hair was as white as milk, who could see only when the sun was shining at mid-day, who could hear only thunder when it rolled in the sky, ate of the roast flag-reeds as if she were starving. She ate a piece of damper with equal joy. Then she said to her daughter: 'Give these good girls, who are our sisters of the Arunta tribe, all they can eat of the young emu, and of the rest.'

As the old grandmother said, so it was done. Then a great peace fell upon Polde. When she had eaten until the flesh of emu and of duck had taken away all care for food, she said to herself, 'Now surely we will get through in safety. For in the very heart of the Red Sand Desert we have found good women of the Arunta tribe, we have found a deep well full of water, and plenty of meat.'

They talked a great deal together after the evening meal. But when Wonka asked how far they were going, Iliapa gave Polde a warning look and quickly replied, 'We have some relations away beyond the dams and the swamp of the Wild Turkey People. We may go as far as that or meet them nearer.' Then Wonka saw that the strangers did not wish to speak of their plans, and no more questions were asked.

When Iliapa had fallen asleep that night, she heard the voice of her boy calling out to her.

'Oh, Alibaka, Alibaka,' she cried out so loud, that she started, and sat up thinking at first that some one had called. But her cheeks were wet with tears, and she knew it was a dream, and that it was her own voice that woke her.

CHAPTER 16

On the morrow, Iliapa got up as usual before the sun rose. She gathered wood, and lighted a fire, to make what was left of the flour into another damper. She and Polde had given all that they had of the last to the women who were so friendly to them, and who had not eaten a morsel of flour bread for many a long day.

When Iliapa had put the damper to bake, she softly woke Polde and the two went a short distance from the camp to have a little talk together.

'You see, Polde,' began Iliapa, 'though the women are friendly, they belong to the Rock-Pigeon Men.' Polde gave a little shudder.

'Yes – I felt very bad,' she said, 'when Wonka told us that. But they are going to stay some days at the Hill of Rocks. We shall be on our way to Labalama before they come back, and, besides, they will never know who touched the Churinga.'

Iliapa shook her head. 'They will track round every inch of ground,' she said slowly, 'until they come to some sand. They will find the mark of your heel in one place, and of my toes in another. They will know they are the marks of two, and that they were made by women. Then they will come together and will say: "It was two women who went into our storehouse. It was two women who touched the holy things, that belong to our fathers of long-ago." How do we know? Perhaps the strange creature that glared at you in the dark may tell them.'

'Let us get away as fast as ever we can,' said Polde, her eyes big with fright.

'That is what I wanted to say. And let us tell nothing of our plans – nothing of Alibaka, or of our going to Labalama.' To this Polde at once agreed.

But when they were eating some food together, Wonka turned to Iliapa, and said to her, 'Do you know some one who is named Alibaka?'

Iliapa was very much taken aback, and not knowing what to say, began to cough as if a crumb had stuck in her throat.

'I will tell you why I ask,' Wonka went on after taking a deep draught out of the pannikin of tea that Polde handed to her, with the view of turning the talk another way. 'Days ago – when the moon was quite young, a white man came to our camp at the Swamp of the Wild Turkey. He had with him a fine black boy, whose name was Alibaka. The man stayed at the Swamp of the Wild Turkey to rest his horses, also to rest the boy, who was tired with so much riding. He got to be friends with my boy Ilbarintja, who left the women's camp last moon, to be with the men.

'One day my boy Ilbarintja came to me and said, "Can we hide Alibaka to-morrow, when the white man goes away?" I said, "Why should we hide him? The white man is kind to him, and gives him a fine horse to ride, all the way to Labalama." But my boy Ilbarintja said to me, "Alibaka cries at night when no one hears him." "Why does he cry at night when no one hears him?" I said, Then Ilbarintja said to me, "Because he wants to get back to his mother, who lives at Balkara. He does not like the white man, who said he was taking him to his father. Now Alibaka is sure this is a lie. So he cries to get back to his mother." Then I said . . . '

Here Wonka's story came to a sudden end. The reason for this was that Polde put down her head and began to cry out loud, like a baby who is badly hurt. But Iliapa sat quite still, though her breath was coming and going in her breast, like the heart-beats of a bird who has been caught when flying in the air.

'What is it? What is it? Do you know this boy Alibaka?' asked Wonka, full of sorrow at Polde's loud grief.

'No! Oh no! I don't know anything about him,' blubbered Polde. 'I was thinking of some fine fat ducks we left behind us. It is such a pity – we may want them so badly before we get to the end of our journey.'

Wonka and Okula began to laugh – even Iliapa smiled a little. It seemed so comical for one to cry at the thought of birds left behind, when she was having a good breakfast.

'Polde is young, and she does not like to go hungry, but she is really quite brave when we are alone,' said Iliapa. She felt very kindly to Polde for her burst of crying at the thought of Alibaka wanting so badly to get back to his mother.

As for herself – Iliapa – she did not know how she kept so quiet. Her heart went on thumping as if it would never get calm. She felt that if she shed even one little tear, she must cry and sob aloud, and tell her whole story. But she kept back her tears and simply asked:

'Then did the black boy go with the man to Labalama?'

'Yes, the white man found out that Alibaka wanted very much to get back to his mother. So then he said that the boy had been given him by his own father.'

'Oh, what a liar that man is!' cried Polde in an angry voice.

'Do you know him?' asked Wonka with surprise.

'No – oh no – but white men who take away black boys so far from their mothers, are always great liars,' replied Polde.

'Well, this man was not cruel to the boy, he seemed proud of him, because he is such a clever rider. He said Alibaka would ride at the races when they got to Labalama, and get a lot of money by being such a fine little jockey. He is a nice boy. He and my Ilbarintja got fond of each other – they were quite sad to part. When I think of my boy, Ilbarintja, I think also of Alibaka. Last night my mother was thirsty. I got up softly to give her some water. While I was up, one of you,' said Wonka, looking from Iliapa to Polde, 'called out Alibaka in your sleep. That made me wonder if you knew this boy.'

Iliapa could not say she did not; yet if she said anything, she must tell all. Then they would know that she and Polde were going straight to Labalama. It would do no harm to tell this to the women. But it might do all the harm in the world, if the Rock-Pigeon Men tracked them, and made sure that they were the two women who had gone into their storehouse, on the Hill of Rocks, and touched the holy things that belonged to their fathers of long-ago. Therefore Iliapa said nothing at all. Seeing this, Polde once more rushed into the breach.

'Very likely I called out Alibaka in my sleep,' she said. 'I have strange dreams. I often dream of people I never saw. I see wild animals too, with more legs than any animals that I ever saw alive.'

'Oh, Polde, see how high the sun has got,' cried Iliapa, who thought of the strange beasts painted in the cave on the Hill of Rocks, and felt afraid that Polde might somehow get into more trouble.

They had now all finished eating. So the two pilgrims made ready to set out on their journey. They filled the water-bag out of the Imanka Well; they left a large piece of damper with the women who had been so kind to them, and these in return gave them a roasted duck. They wanted also to give them a piece of the emu, but Iliapa said they had enough to take them across the rest of the Red Sand Desert, and they did not want to carry an ounce more than they needed.

Wonka and Okula went with them a mile or so of the way, leaving the baby asleep with the grandmother. They parted at last, with many wishes that they might meet again, and spend some days together.

'If only they did not belong to the Rock-Pigeon Men, how glad I would have been to tell them all,' said Iliapa. 'When Wonka spoke of my boy crying to come back to me – oh, it was as if some one was beating me hard with a stone,' she added.

Then she sat down and cried for a little. Not loud, nor sobbing, but with tears running fast one after the other down her cheeks. After that she felt better, and they both walked on with long, fast strides, until the sand again became soft and deep and heavy. By mid-day all trace of trees had quite disappeared. They found a rock with many loose stones lying about. In the shadow of this rock they lay down and slept for some hours. Then they drank some water, ate a little food, and walked on in the starlight.

They camped for the night in a narrow gully that had a few low creeping bushes along the sides. Some of these had withered, and they used them for making the water boil for tea. They had come nearly to the last of the tea and sugar. But they had also come nearly to the last of the Red Sand Desert, and this made them feel light of heart. Now on any day they might meet the men and the camels that were taking goods to Antaka and Balkara and other stations.

After they lay down, Polde began the old story: 'Ah, what a fine day that will be . . . ' But Iliapa cried out like one in pain: 'Don't, don't say that! It makes me think too much of Alibaka crying to come back to me. I do not want to cry. I want to sleep well, to be strong and to rise early, so as to hurry on, till we get to the end.'

CHAPTER 17

Before the day broke next morning, a great sandstorm set in. Iliapa was first awakened by a strange deep whistling sound, that seemed to be a great way off. As it came nearer this deepened to a great roar. Sometimes it was like the trampling of thousands of wild cattle, then like the fierce rush of mighty waters.

'What can it be?' said Iliapa, as Polde started up in much alarm.

'It is a storm of the desert,' replied Polde. 'Roll up all your things fast round you, and turn your face to the ground.'

Even as she was speaking, the hurricane came rushing down the gully carrying clouds of sand, tearing up shrubs and withered grass, and hurling sticks and stones in every direction, like a creature that has gone mad with anger.

When the storm was at its worst, the noise was simply deafening. It was as if a hundred wild voices were all shrieking together, each trying to rise above the others.

When at last there was a lull, Iliapa heard Polde's voice as if at some distance. She felt for her, where she should be lying, but Polde was not there.

'Where are you?' she cried out at the pitch of her voice. It was still impossible to see, for all the sky was dark, and the air thick with sand and dust, with leaves and sticks and battered twigs. Another gust came tearing along, and it was no use trying to speak until this was over. When it became calmer, Iliapa heard Polde once more, crying out tearfully, 'Has the storm taken you away?'

'No, I am all right,' cried Iliapa, as loud as she could shout. She was afraid to move, least the wind should carry away some of the things that she had put under her so as to keep them safe.

At last the storm died away and daylight crept into the sky.

Iliapa rose up slowly, still fearing that some sudden rush of wind might all at once carry her off her feet. Peering about on all sides, after a few minutes, she saw Polde a little way below in the gully, crouching up against a draggled heap of bushes, her netted bag, her blanket, her digging-stick, and other belongings lying round her in wild disorder against some bushes.

She tried to tell Iliapa how she had come there. But it was like a dream to her, full of furious noises. She had been in sandstorms before, but this had been worse than any of them. Before the storm had got to its height, she thought she would like to be a little nearer to Iliapa. Folding the blanket round her, and keeping fast hold of the other things, she half rose. The next moment she was hurled by the wind down the side of the gully, as if she were a handful of withered grass.

'But I did not let the things go,' she said with some pride, 'and when I came against the bushes, I stuck here and tried to call out to you. But I was like a little swallow, that has no feathers, spitting at thunder. I thought to myself: "What if Iliapa was carried away by the wind, and put down some hole, head first, deep down." And then do you know what I thought, Iliapa?'

Iliapa laughed, and said how could she know what came into Polde's head, even when there was no storm.

'Well, what I thought was that the Rock-Pigeon Men were working magic against us; that we would be hurt and made ill and lame, and that then they would catch up to us.'

'But, you see, we are all right – we have only a few scratches. We can make an early start after we eat and drink, and before the sun is high in the sky we shall be out of the Red Sand Desert,' said Iliapa, speaking brightly and going to look for sticks to boil the water.

She would not like to tell Polde how much she feared what might happen to them, through having touched and looked at things that were forbidden to all women and children of the Arunta people, upon pain of death, or of punishment that was almost worse than death.

Having lit the fire, she got the quart pot, and then stood staring about with a face full of fear.

'Polde – the water-bag,' she gasped.

'The water-bag?' echoed Polde. Then she stood as if all courage had gone from her. It was one of the things she had carried and now it was nowhere to be seen.

'Did you have it when you got up and the storm blew you over?' asked Iliapa.

'Did I have it when I was blown over? Oh, I cannot think – I cannot think,' said Polde. Then she covered her face with her hands and cried. She had had sense enough to call out to Iliapa what she should do, but the shrieking sound all round had been so much more frightful than any storm she had been in before, she felt she must be nearer Iliapa. And this was what came of being a coward.

'Don't cry, Polde, don't cry,' said Iliapa in a coaxing tone.

The fact was that she herself was almost on the point of breaking down. For if the water-bag was lost or spoiled, it would be the greatest piece of bad luck that could happen to them. She would not face the thought.

'Let us look for it with great care, all the way down to the bottom of the gully. It was carried away like a stick, or a handful of dried leaves. But we'll find it against a bush, or perhaps at the other side.'

Not a bush, not a corner, not a crevice did they miss in that long painful search. The sun mounted up strong and fierce, and still they searched and searched, while the sweat poured from them, as if they were out in a shower of blinding rain.

The cruel north-east wind began to blow, when they guessed it was about two hours before mid-day. By that time they were so thirsty, that they could hardly speak. Should they get to the next water that night? And if not, how long could they live without a drop to wet their lips?

While the sun was at its worst, nothing was left for them to do, except to lie down in the shade of some bushes. Polde after a little time fell fast asleep. But Iliapa had the feeling, that if she once fell asleep, she might never wake again. It was not only the loss of the bag, with all the water they had. This was so bad in itself, that it might mean death from thirst. But besides this, there was the great vague fear of evil magic, worked by the Rock-Pigeon Men.

Old stories came back to her, that she had heard as a child, of the awful things that were done by magic. How men changed into eagles, and came flying to their enemies to pick out their eyes and their hearts, with cruel beaks and long sharp claws. How by a spell, even the face of the country was at times changed, so that where to-night there were great ridges of sand, groups of bushes and lines of watercourses, in the morning there was nothing but a wide plain of sand, in which all sign of the right way to go was lost for ever.

While this was passing through her mind, Iliapa chanced to look at the spot on which they had camped, on reaching the gully last night.

It had been a smooth space on the gully side, with nothing but bushes and tall tufts of dry white grass. Now there was not a single blade of grass to be seen, and sand lay piled high around the bushes. What if the water-bag was buried under this sand?

She left Polde asleep, and crept up to the bushes with the sand heaped up around them. She felt so weak with thirst, and fear and misery, that it seemed as if she had not strength left for searching. However, she sat down as near as she could guess, in the place where Polde had slept. She plunged her hands into the sand, and turned it over from side to side. No – there was nothing here but dry sand.

'I have searched it all,' she thought, 'from one side to the other. It is useless; the wild wind took it up like a feather and carried it away high up in the air for miles and miles. And now what can we do? Can I even walk a few miles to look for a water-hole, or a dam, or a native well?'

Iliapa stood up, as these thoughts passed through her mind, and found that her legs were trembling beneath her. For the first time a feeling of being quite helpless came over her. She lay down and moaned, rolling her head from side to side. She felt something hard against her neck. She sat up and pressed her hands through the sand once more. It was the nozzle of the water-bag that she had felt, where it lay deep in the sand.

Yes! There it was safe and sound, full of water.

So great was her relief, that for a little time she could hardly believe her eyes. But after slowly drinking half a pannikinful out of the bag, Iliapa felt once more that they were safe. She went to tell Polde the joyful news. But when she saw her so fast asleep, when she saw how high the sun was in the sky, and felt so tired in every limb, that she knew that she could do nothing until she, too, had rested, she put all their things safe between her and Polde, and lay down. In a few minutes she was fast asleep.

The sun was setting when she woke, and for some minutes she could not make out where they were, or how they came there, or what had taken place. Her head was very giddy, and she was aching all over.

She heard Polde moving and giving a great sigh, then saying in a weak voice: 'No water, no water.'

This cleared up Iliapa's mind. 'Yes, yes, Polde, we have water, I found the bag buried under the sand.'

She felt for it, and poured out a full pannikin for Polde, who swallowed the whole to the last drop, without a pause.

After they had had something to eat they decided it would be best to camp in the gully, and make a fresh start at the first peep of dawn.

For the first time, they had lost a day, and camped for a second night in the same place.

CHAPTER 18

You could hardly tell black from white, in the faint dawn, when Polde got up and made the fire. She had slept so much the day before that she could sleep no longer. She heard a call like that of a shining dove, and went to see if there could really be one near. But no bird was to be seen. She made tea, and then called Iliapa.

They got away before the sun rose, and about mid-day they came within sight of the wooded country that stretched beyond the Red Sand Desert. These three long days, that had been so full of weariness and fear and care, were as if quite put aside by Polde, when at last they left the desert behind them, and reached a group of tall stringy-bark trees. They had just enough damper left to make their mid-day meal.

So as Polde made the fire, to boil the water, she kept on half chanting a song that she made up as she went along: 'Oh, what a fine day for us – what a fine day for us. We have left behind a land that has no food for man nor beast, without bird or leaf. Oh, what a fine day. We have come to a country that has trees and grass and water-holes, and dams and creeks and wells; a country that has birds in the trees and fish in the water and tracks without spinifex. Oh, what a fine day for us,' etc., etc.

They rested and slept for three hours, and then went on their way, expecting to reach a dam not far from the telegraph line, about sunset. But before long Polde began to see that they could not be on the right way. She saw a line of hills in the distance, away to the right, that she had not seen when she had made this journey before. When she first sighed this line, it was so faint and blue, she thought it must be a low bank of clouds.

'But clouds do not stay all the time in one place,' she thought, as she looked hard at this line, and saw that instead of passing away, it looked more firm.

'Is that where the dam is, where we are going to sit down?' asked Iliapa, when at last, close on sundown, Polde stood still, looking away to the right, and now quite sure that it really was a line of hills.

'Iliapa, we have come out of the way, we have kept too much to the right. I have been stupid,' said Polde in a humble sort of way.

'Then we must keep more to the left,' said Iliapa, hiding her dismay. 'See, away there to the left, is there not a lake with trees round it?'

'No – no – that is the make-believe,' replied Polde, using the native word for mirage. Yet in the glow of the sunset, the water and the trees looked so lifelike, that it was hard to believe it was a kind of picture that would soon fade away.

Nearer at hand, however, than the blue hills or the idle mirage, there were groups of dwarf gum- and box-trees. They marked the course of a creek whose dry bed widened out here and there into what had been a short time before large pools of water. But though these were now also dried up by the fierce summer sun, yet the bottom ground was a little damp still.

'If we dig,' said Polde, 'the water will rise.' She was beginning to do this, when they heard the cries of water-fowl overhead. Wherever there is water found, there do the fowls of the air and the creatures of the earth gather together. Therefore both at once stood up and eagerly watched the flight of the birds. They flew along the course of the creek to the left, alighting among some trees that looked to be about a couple of miles away.

They at once agreed it would be best to go there, as they would not only be sure of water, but also have more chance of killing some bird or beast for supper. The sky was cloudless, and the stars were out all over it, when they started for the trees to which the wild-fowl had flown.

It took them a good deal longer to get there than they expected. But they walked along the bed of the creek, and found it smooth and firm, compared with the drifting sand of the desert.

They were right in making sure of water, where the wild ducks and swans had found a resting-place. There was a grand big pool, with trees, rushes, and sedges growing round. The water was so cool and sweet, and they were so thirsty – they drank so much that it seemed as if they need not look for any more supper.

'If we go to sleep now, we shall awake before daylight, and hunt down a duck or something before the sun gets up,' said Iliapa. Polde, who was very tired, and felt loath to begin to scramble for game in the dark, said yes to this. Still she felt rather sad, when she thought how good a roasted bird would taste, after having had nothing to eat for many long hours.

'If we only had a little flour left, I would make a nice bright fire, and Iliapa would make another damper,' she thought. But there was no flour, so it was no use making a fire. Indeed, Iliapa had already curled herself up for the night under a desert oak. Polde was on the point of doing the same, when she heard the cries of some wild swans coming to the pool.

They came slowly down, quite near the bank on which the two had camped. But one of them, in place of getting on the bosom of the pool, fell heavily on the ground, not more than five or six yards from where Polde was sitting. Whether it had got some hurt, or had become exhausted with a long flight over waterless sands, it would be hard to say. But when it tried to rise from the ground, flapping its wide wings in a vain attempt at flying, it fell over on its side.

This was a grand chance for Polde. In a very few minutes it was no longer a bird, but the body of one, and she was lighting a fire on which to cook it. 'It is not very fat,' she said as she cut it up, so that it might roast all the quicker; 'but it is not old either, so it will not be tough.'

She was right in this, and it turned out to be a good thing for them, that the swan was so large, that they ate only about a quarter of it that night. As soon as they had done eating, they both lay down and in a few minutes were fast asleep.

It was barely midnight, however, when Iliapa was wakened by some noises, that seemed to be quite near them. She started up, and at first seeing Polde fast asleep, she thought it had been, not real, but something in a dream. Next minute, however, she heard a man's voice distinctly calling out, 'Ampa, Ampa.' Then a voice at some distance answered back.

They were people of the Arunta tribe. Could they be the Rock-Pigeon Men? 'Polde, Polde, wake up, wake up,' said Iliapa in a low whisper, grasping her by the arm. Polde woke up as quickly as a collie dog. At the same instant, a few hundred yards away they both saw a fire flare up, as if some brushwood were set alight. This was quickly followed by volumes of smoke, as if heavier wood were put on the fire. They heard a sound of voices, and saw three men sitting round the fire. In a few minutes, the smell of singed feathers and of roasting flesh reached them.

Then they knew that these men, whoever they were, had made a night march, to reach the water-hole, and were now getting their supper ready.

'Can it be the Rock-Pigeon Men,' whispered Polde in a voice shaking with fear. The same dread filled Iliapa's mind and for a little time took away from her the power of speech. Perhaps they had hurried back, the moment they found the storehouse on the Hill of Rocks had been touched. Men were so much stronger than women – they might have kept on walking night and day, once they found the tracks of women.

'We lost so much time through the storm in the Red Sand Desert,' said Polde, staring at the fire, and the men sitting round it, as if she could not take her eyes off them. But already Iliapa was gathering up their things. In a few minutes they were creeping away round by the southern side of the pool. The men were camped on the northern side.

Here they stood for a moment, while Polde looked at some of the big stars to make out the course they should take.

'We have forgotten to fill the water-bag,' whispered Polde. It was a lucky thing that she thought of this. They filled the bag, and then fled for their lives, walking and running, until the moon had set, and the stars began to turn pale.

At dawn they were so much knocked up that they could walk no further, until they had slept and rested. They found a sheltered spot under some tall straggling salt-bushes. Here they lay down and fell at once into a profound sleep.

CHAPTER 19

'What is the matter with you, Iliapa? Are you not well?' were Polde's first words on awakening next morning. When she first looked round, she could see nothing of Iliapa. But on getting up from the shelter of the salt-bushes, she found her on the other side, sitting down with her back to the east, covering her face with both hands.

Iliapa did not reply or look up. Then a great fear fell upon Polde.

'Iliapa has fallen ill,' she thought. 'She cannot speak or walk, or look up. If she dies and leaves me alone, oh, what will become of me? The Rock-Pigeon Men may be, even now, tracking us from the water-hole of the wild-fowl.'

The thought of this was too much for Polde. She threw herself on the ground, and began to weep aloud. This at once roused Iliapa.

'What makes you cry like that, Polde? Are you hungry? Or what can it be that makes you so foolish?' she asked in a vexed tone.

'Do I only cry when I am hungry or thirsty? Is that all I care for – what I eat and drink? Was that what made me come away with you from Antaka? See now what a fool I was to come, for you only throw hard words at me, as you throw stones at a dog.'

Polde spoke very fast and very loud, until she came to the last words, when she choked and sobbed again.

'Me throw hard words at you, Polde? Oh, no, no,' Iliapa answered softly. 'Why, Polde, you are the best friend I have in the world. What should I have done without you? My bones would lie, before this, getting white in the sun, if you had not come with me. It makes me bad to hear you cry. Tell me what has hurt you?'

'I get up,' cried Polde, dashing the tears from her eyes, 'and I cannot see you. I look round, you are sitting there on the ground, with your face in your hands as if you cared no more to look at the sun. I speak to you, I ask like a sister, "Are you well?" You do not move, you do not speak a word or lift an eye. Then my bowels shake within me from fear. I say to myself, "Iliapa is ill; she will die and leave me alone." At that I cry aloud. Then you move, you lift your eyes, you speak. But what do you say? "Are you hungry, or are you a fool, that you cry like this?" If you are tired of me, leave me here to the Rock-Pigeon Men, and go to your boy.'

'Leave you to the Rock-Pigeon Men?' echoed Iliapa, her voice trembling. 'Polde, I would die first. I will tell you what I was thinking of so much, when you spoke and I did not hear. I was blind and I was deaf because my mind went to a day long ago when my father saved so many from dying of thirst and hunger. Now I am trying to remember a spell that might help us too.'

'Do you know one? What is it? Will you work it now?' asked Polde, throwing aside in a moment all that had vexed her.

'Let me be for a little time alone. By-and-by I will tell you.' Iliapa sat as before, fronting the west.

It is true of black people as of the white races, that the mind is a house of many mansions. In these are countless thoughts and happenings that are forgotten in ordinary life, till some connecting link is touched, and the by-gone events and emotions spring to the surface of memory with curious vividness. It was thus with Iliapa, when beset with terror of the Rock-Pigeon Men. The terror of being killed, before she could rescue her boy, brought back to her a time that had lain forgotten for many a day.

She was a small child famishing for the want of food and water – especially water. The land was stricken by a great drought that had lapped up, one by one, the lakes, the creeks and the native wells. At last, her people reached a spring which gushed out from the bowels of the earth, and was never known to run dry. Here they had plenty of beasts and birds, that like themselves had come from afar to what was the last refuge in a great tract of country. But in the third summer of the drought, the spring, which was known as the Never-Dry-Pool, began slowly to sink away. Day by day its hidden sources shrank, as if touched by the might of the sun, that raged in the sky from morning till night like a wizard fire, kept alive by consuming all the moisture that was to be found in the land.

Only a small ration of water was allowed to each. So small that at last the youngest and the oldest, and the more weakly were in a dying state. Erungara and the older men went through many ceremonies to call down the rain that would save them. Here Iliapa's memory became dim. But the last thing that took place stood out before her like a picture. Her father was lying down ill. The people helped him to stand up. He was striped all over with white clay and ochre. The skins of beasts were heaped round his feet. Some of the older men held him up, while he made strange signals heavenward. He uttered low growling sounds to make thunder roll in the sky, and cut zigzag lines with both hands as a call for lightning. That night a great thunderstorm was followed by a deluge of rain.

It was after recalling these events that Iliapa asked herself whether there was not some spell she could work for the overthrow of the enemies, who were most likely coming nearer every hour. She sat on motionless as a mother-swallow hatching eggs, her head bent, her face covered with both hands. 'Yes, the Arungquiltha,' she said at last half-aloud, her face lit up with a glow of hope.

Polde in the meantime had gone on her way scanning the country around. She could see no place that was likely to have anything in it alive. A hill to the south-east caught her eye. She looked at it for some moments, then walked swiftly on. When she got nearer she saw it was a rise of strange shape with some desert oaks on the top. 'Yes – it is the very one – it is the Hill of the Cave.' She spent some time in examining it, but did not climb to the top. Then she hastened back to Iliapa. She found her standing up, looking fixedly towards the north.

'Look at the hill away there,' said Polde, pointing to it. 'There is a large cave in it where my brother-in-law Parinja hid for three days and three nights when the Grass-Seed Men were after him. No one else knew the cave was there – only Parinja. We passed quite close to it when we three went to Labalama, where my man died.'

'A cave – a hiding-place, and no one knows of it,' said Iliapa. 'Come and let us see what it is like.'

While Iliapa was speaking, they had gathered up their things, and, having each drunk half a pannikin of water, they set out as fast as their legs could carry them for the Hill of the Cave.

It was close on mid-day when they reached it. The first thing was to find the cave. For a time it seemed that there was not such a thing near the place. The hill was cone-shaped at the top, steep on one side, sloping on the other. On the sloping side there were trees and bushes, with large rocks jutting out here and there. The steep side was quite bare and very stony.

The two looked all over both sides from top to bottom – peering under each bush, feeling every rock to see if it would move. But they found no sign of an opening.

'Perhaps it is not the hill you mean,' said Iliapa, who grudged every moment of time they lost.

'Yes, yes, I am sure this is the hill,' replied Polde. 'If you stand up here, I will show you why I am quite sure.'

They were then on the top of the hill, having come there again, after searching it all over. As Polde spoke, she stepped on a large smooth stone and pointed southward. Iliapa stood up beside her, and looked over a plain that was in parts well-wooded, but almost entirely bare of grass. Across this plain, the channel of a creek was well-marked in all its windings by pieces of snow-white quartz. In places, this was so regular, that it looked like a thin stream of milk. As the ground on each side was dark, the effect was too strange to be mistaken.

'That is the White Stone Creek,' said Polde. 'We followed it from here, till we came to the White Stone Water-hole. Near this hill, Parinja pointed it out, and told us about the cave. But what has become of it?'

Polde gave a longing look towards the south. The country was so much easier to get over than the way had been up to this. There were no hills of hot sand, no stones and spinifex to cut their feet. Before the sun went down they could reach the White Stone Water-hole, where they would get plenty to eat, where they could bathe and rest, and then go on by the iron poles. Once they struck these, they might at any hour meet Hussein with the caravan of camels.

'Let us eat here, and then go on as fast as we can,' she said. But Iliapa shook her head.

'If the Rock-Pigeon Men are tracking us, they might catch up to us before the sun goes down,' she replied. 'I told you that I was calling back things of long-ago. There was an old woman in our camp once who was very wise. She knew how to do harm to her enemies, and how to do good to her friends. When I was a little girl, I followed her one day into the woods, and saw what she did, and heard what she said. She was half blind, so I could go quite near her without being seen. I must sing the words, and work the spell alone before the sun goes down. As soon as you spoke of the cave, I thought that is where we can hide until the Rock-Pigeon Men come to harm, or turn back. There are some little things that I must make. My father sometimes allowed Alibaka to have them to play with, so that they are quite clear in my mind. They were the things the old wise woman used. Though she could not bring down rain as my father did when we were all dying of thirst and hunger, yet every one knew she could work this charm, and I believe I can.'

Polde, who had been standing on the smooth rock, drinking in every word spoken by Iliapa, now stepped on to the ground. In doing this, she stumbled a little and to save herself from falling, she leant heavily on its edge. To her surprise, it moved under her.

'See, Iliapa,' she cried. 'I can move it. I thought it grew here and belonged to the earth.'

Iliapa at once looked all round the rock. At first, it seemed as if it were rooted in the earth. Yet, when the leaned hard on the outer edge, it certainly moved. They loosened the earth around it and lo! they found it was no rock. It was a great flat stone, that had been placed over the opening to a cave.

There were some smaller stones that had been built up in a cunning way at one side. They removed these, and found an opening large enough for one to squeeze through.

'But what if it is another storehouse?' said Iliapa. 'What if there are more holy things in here?'

'Let us look all round to make sure,' said Polde. 'Parinja, my man's brother, said he found it out by himself, and that no one knew of it. He thought it was made as a hiding-place, in the far long-ago.'

Iliapa slipped in by the side opening, Polde close behind. When their eyes got used to the gloom, which was only broken by the light that came in at the side, they found it was a good roomy cave, much larger than the storehouse on the Hill of Rocks. They could stand up in it without touching the roof, and there were hidden places apart from the opening in the side, through which a little light and air came in.

They struck some matches and peered all round. They found no trace of any Churinga. But in one corner, there were some bunches of the red-barred tail-feathers of the black cockatoo, a Chilara, or head-band of a curious kind, also an Ikura, a very strong sort of fibre bag. Both these Iliapa knew at once to be of the kind that her father used to have.

'There seems to have been no one near the place for a long time, and it was never a storehouse,' she said. 'Now we have a safe hiding-place, let us put our things in here at once.'

When they had done so, they sat on the hill-top and ate a portion of the swan. Then Iliapa began to work the spell as she had seen and heard the very Wise Old Woman work it so many years before.

First she took a small stick, and with her clasp-knife fashioned it as well as she could into the shape of a tiny knife-blade. To the blunt end of this she fixed a piece of the grass resin, and fastened it to a slender bit of stick, sharpened at one end, to make it look like a tiny spear. The next thing was to make a spear-thrower, on the same scale as the spear and the wooden knife-blade. Then she bored a hole in the spear-thrower, just large enough to make the end of the baby spear fit into it quite tightly. The last thing was to paint this all over with red ochre, and put them in the sum to dry.

'What did you say it is called?' asked Polde, who had looked on with deep interest, full of wonder at the quick, clever way in which Iliapa had made and fixed these small articles together.'

'Arungquiltha,' replied Iliapa. 'But do not ask me anything about it. Now I must go and sing over it alone, and leave it in the sun.'

'Let me come with you. I will stay so far away, that I cannot hear you,' pleaded Polde.

So she stayed at a little distance, when Iliapa went to the foot of the hill, and sang certain words over the Arungquiltha, the gist of them being, 'Go straight, go straight and kill them.'

She repeated this four times before the sun set.

Polde did not go with her the last time, for she had found and killed a large snake, and was busy cooking it for an evening meal. They kept what was left of the swan for the journey to the White Stone Water-hole.

'If the Rock-Pigeon Men came on our tracks, they would be here by this time,' said Iliapa when the sun had gone down. All the sky in the west was flaming, as if set in a blaze by the sun in going out of sight. They could see it was going to be very hot on the morrow, and made up their minds to start for the White Stone Water-hole at daybreak.

'After that the way will be easy,' said Iliapa. 'Then when some suns rise and set at last, at last, I shall see my boy.'

It was not yet dark, when they lay down, close by the opening into the cave.

CHAPTER 20

It was after midnight when Iliapa was awakened by Polde crying out in a loud voice, 'The sharp red spear, the sharp red spear. Oh, it is flying after me.'

'Polde, Polde, what are you saying? What is the matter with you?' said Iliapa in a low voice.

'If it touches me I am killed,' said Polde in a trembling voice. She was sitting up now, with her eyes wide open. She had been dreaming, and the dream was so real to her that for a few minutes she could not believe that it was a dream.

'You frighten me so much, crying out in that way. At first, I made sure it must be the Rock-Pigeon Men come down upon us,' said Iliapa. 'Perhaps it was the little red spear of the Arungquiltha that put it into your head.'

'I saw it flying at me through the air, sharper than the claw of an old kangaroo, just as I see you at this moment,' replied Polde.

They were now wide awake, both feeling rather restless and excited. Iliapa got up, and stood looking to the south, thinking of her boy with all her heart, yearning for the hour when she could once more throw her arms round him, and take him to herself. Where would she first see him? And would that evil man, Simon, try to keep them apart?

But he dared not. There were other white people who were good and kind; there was the doctor, for whom she had a letter from Antaka. As she thought of it, she put her hand on the little silk bag that was tied by a cord round her neck.

'Iliapa, Iliapa, look, oh look,' said Polde in a hoarse whisper. She pointed to the plain that lay to the north, without hill or trees. There, quite visible in the moon and starlight were three people walking quickly towards the hill.

'The Rock-Pigeon Men!' gasped Iliapa in a small weak voice. For a little time the sight of these three, coming each moment nearer, took away from her the power of speech, almost of thought. Polde, drawing closer to her, tried to think of some word of courage. But she, too, was as if stricken dumb. Then with an effort she said: 'It is good we have the cave.'

On came the men with long, fast strides. As they came near the Hill of the Cave, the two forlorn women, who were watching them in dumb despair, could see quite clearly that they were black men, almost naked, each carrying spears, a bag and a shield.

'Yes, we have the cave – we have the cave to hide in,' said Iliapa, rousing herself from the dismay that had fallen on her. Though, from the first moment of seeing the men, at the Hill of Rocks, she had feared they were the Rock-Pigeon Men looking for them, yet it had been but a fear. Now when the first terror passed away, her courage came back. She thought how hard it had been to find the opening to the cave, even when they searched for it knowing that it was there. These men knew nothing of it. Then she thought of the Arungquiltha fixed out there to do them some mischief, and the thought, strange to say, revived her courage so that she made up her mind not to lose hope, but try to feel sure that the two of them would somehow get safely away.

'They have tracked us from our last camping-place; but they will not find the opening by which we came in. Can we quite close it up from the inside, as it was before?' said Polde, keeping fear out of her voice as well as she could. As sometimes happens with those who are quickly moved by trifles, a great danger seemed to steady her nerves.

'Of course we can,' replied Iliapa, as they went into the cave. And in the moonlight that streamed in, she showed Polde how well the stones they had moved, fitted into their place. The big smooth stone on top, that looked like a solid part of the hill, lapped over and above these stones, so that it was hardly possible the cave should be found by anyone who did not know it was there.

They crouched down in it, listening intently for any sound. But they heard none.

'Perhaps they have gone on,' said Iliapa, at last. Polde, overcome with fatigue and anxiety, had fallen fast asleep. As the hours wore on, Iliapa also dozed from time to time. But, with a great effort, she kept herself awake. At last, she made up her mind that she would creep out carefully to see whether the men had camped near the hill, or were anywhere to be seen.

She removed the stones, and went out with as little noise as a fish swims. She found that the dawn was red in the east, so she did not stand up, until she had watched for some time to make sure that there was no one in sight. Then, keeping well within cover as she moved, she looked up and down the sides of the hill.

Yes, there they were, the three of them, fast asleep, in a hollow on the sloping side of the hill. Even as she looked, one of them moved and half rose. Iliapa dropped on the ground, till she saw him lying down again. But she knew it would not be long before they would be astir. As soon, therefore, as she got back to the cave, her first care was to close up the opening, as carefully as it was closed when they found it.

When she saw by the light that came in through some crevices, that the sun was rising, she woke Polde, and told her what she had seen.

'Then they are quite near us?' said Polde in a whisper. 'If only your Arungquiltha would make lightning from the sky come down and strike them dead,' she added, dwelling on the thought with some comfort.

'When they do not find our tracks going on, they may think that we have gone back,' returned Iliapa, trying hard to keep up their spirits, thankful and even wondering a little that Polde kept so calm,.

The minutes dragged on like hours, as they sat and waited in the furthest recess of the cave. What were the men doing now? Would they stay long? Would they come on the top of the hill and search about like hunters after game? Would they search and search, until they found that the stones under the big round flat rock could be moved, and that there was a cave beyond?

The sun had been up some hours, when the men came into the shade of the trees on top of the hill, and stood talking close to the big stone that covered the cave opening.

'They were here only last night,' said one of them. 'That is plain from the ashes, and the backbone of the snake they ate!'

'They had more than a snake,' said another. 'Look at this, it is the wing-bone of a big swan.'

There was dead silence for a few moments. Then one said, 'Are we on the wrong tracks? How could two women, flying alone, catch a swan? Even a man has to be a cunning hunter before he can do that, without a gun.'

'We cannot be on the wrong tracks,' replied another. 'We have come after them straight on from the Hill of Rocks, where they dared to enter our storehouse, where they treated the holy things of our forefathers like bits of old bark lying under a tree. We followed them on from our camp, through the Red Sand Desert, and up the Ti-tree Creek.'

'There is something strange about them,' said the first man. He was walking about at a little distance from the rest, and the trembling women in the cave could not hear all he said.

But they heard another say, as if in answer,

'Yes, it is true that an evil spirit sometimes leads people on the wrong tracks as if to destroy them. If they came here last night, where can they be? We have searched all round, but found nothing at all to show that they left this hill.'

There was some more talk, which neither Iliapa nor Polde could hear, as the men had moved away to the side of the hill. At the end of a few minutes they came back, and one of them sat on the big smooth stone.

'Yes, if you like,' he said. 'I will stay here and keep watch. They may have found a hole somewhere near, from which they could see which way we went. If we had not found the Arungquiltha here, we could not be sure that they knew we were after them. I do not like the look of that charm – there is danger in it.'

There was some further talk, before two of them went away to make a close search all round, and to find some animal to kill to eat. They had also to get some water, and they spoke of a secret well that was a short way from the hill.

'If we cannot get them to-night, we must find them to-morrow, or give up and turn back,' said the man who was sitting on the stone.

'Oh, yes we'll get them all right. They may be quite near us at this moment,' said one of the two who were going to search.

'And when we catch them, shall we put their eyes out with a fire-stick, or kill them on the spot?' asked the man who was sitting on the stone.

Iliapa felt Polde trembling all over, like a leaf in the wind, and for a moment placed her hand on her mouth, fearing she might not be able to keep from screaming. But, as Polde afterwards said, 'My tongue was so dead with fright, I could not even move it to wet my lips.'

They sat silent as if turned to stone, feeling that they were within a hair's-breadth of death – or worse. Then again the thought of the

Arungquiltha revived Iliapa's drooping courage.

'If they find us,' whispered Polde, at last, 'I hope they will kill us on the spot. If they put our eyes out, it will take us many a day and many a night to die of hunger and thirst. There was a woman. . . . '

'Don't, Polde, don't speak of that fearful story,' whispered Iliapa. 'I tell you they will not get us. If you go on thinking of the evil that may come, the fear will make us weak. I know that I am going to get to my boy, and that you are going to help me all the way, and that the Arungquiltha will help us both.'

After this, they sat without saying a word, until a soft buzzing kind of sound made itself heard.

'What can it be?' said Iliapa.

'Perhaps he is searching about near the side of the stone, where the opening is,' said Polde.

'No, no. It is not a sound like that,' replied Iliapa. 'You might as well say it was thunder.'

They listened again so intently that they hardly breathed.

'I know what it is,' said Iliapa at last. 'The man who stayed to watch, has gone to sleep, and is snoring.'

'Are you quite sure?' asked Polde, whose senses were not quite as keen as Iliapa's.

Iliapa, by way of reply, went to the opening and carefully removed one of the stones. The opening thus made was just large enough for her to put her head and neck through. But this was enough to let her see that she was not mistaken. The man was lying by the stone, fast asleep, one arm under his head, the other resting on his spear, overcome by the fatigue of a long forced marching, and a wounded foot.

'Look,' she said to Polde.

Polde stared for a long time, as if unable to take her eyes away from the sight.

'Could we not kill him in his sleep?' she whispered at last, a fierce light in her big black eyes. 'The other two would get such a fright, they would run away for their lives,' she went on.

Iliapa sat for some moments without stirring, or saying a word.

'We could kill him quite well,' urged Polde in a thick voice, pointing first to the heavy stone they had removed from the opening, and then to the man who lay fast alseep. 'Or would the tomahawk split his head better?' In this supreme hour the savage got the upper hand of Polde. She asked the question gloating on the thought. But Iliapa shuddered.

'It would be too ugly,' she said. 'There would be no joy in getting to Alibaka if we killed a man on the way.'

'And what joy will we have if they put out our eyes with fire-sticks and leave us to starve like baby crows that have no mother? The tomahawk will be best. I know how to strike behind the ear – you need not touch him.' Polde rose as if to get the tomahawk out of her bag. But Iliapa held her hand.

'We may never get away alive,' pleaded Polde. 'Already they think there is something strange at work. When they come back and find the man they left here dead, they will say the Arungquiltha or some strong magic is working for us. They would never know that he was killed when asleep. This may be the great good worked by your spell – the last one chance of our lives. Let me.' Iliapa sat without moving or speaking as if tempted to give way. But when Polde drew the axe out of her bag, Iliapa suddenly cried out: 'No, no, Polde. Let us get ready to fly to-night when they go to sleep. I know what we must do.' She rose as she spoke.

Giving a careful look at the man to make sure he was still fast asleep, she removed the other two stones from the opening, slipped out, and going a short distance away, pulled up several handfuls of porcupine grass that grew here and there over the hill-top in thick tussocks.

Polde watched her in stupefied wonder. The thought crossed her mind that perhaps Iliapa had, all at once, gone a little mad. If the man had just opened his eyes while she was out there, would he not jump up and spear her to death on the spot? And why should she risk her life for a few handfuls of withered grass?

Iliapa sped back to the cave as quietly as a shadow. Having closed the opening, all but one stone, she went to the further end, and got the bunches of feathers that were lying there. These, and the strong grass in her lap, she began to weave together, into what looked like a slender flat mat. She sat up against the hole through which the light came, and worked away with lightning quickness, while Polde looked on till light dawned on her.

'Are you make kuditcha shoes, Iliapa?'

'Yes; you know you must not be able to tell the heel from the toes; and now I must get some of my hair, to bind the feathers and the grass together.'

Iliapa took a little sheaf of hair, on the right side of her head, and wound it twice round her very slender right hand, Then she pulled with all her might, until she pulled it all out by the roots. It was thick, strong hair. There were over four hundred hairs in all, which she divided into strands, allowing twenty hairs to each.

This gave her twenty strands, and ten hairs left over. With these strands she wove and tied the feathers and grass so tightly together, that it was plain it would take some time to wear them out.

In a much shorter time than it took her to make the first shoe, Iliapa made the second. She had just enough hair, using the strand that had only ten in it, to finish the second shoe. Then she pulled out another sheaf of hair for the next pair, dividing it in the same way.

'Now, Polde, get that ball of opossum fur string, and fasten some of it to these shoes. You see, there must be strings from behind the heels, and strings from the middle, to fasten round your feet.'

'Are these for me? Oh, Iliapa, how good they are, and how fast you made them,' said Polde, holding up the sandals – for that is what they were, rather than shoes – and looking at them all over.

Iliapa made no answer, for by this time she was deep in working at the second pair, those that she herself would wear. She could not work without light, and, of course, as soon as the man who slept awoke, or the other two returned, this stone must be fitted into its place, and they would be in darkness until the moment came when they could get away. 'The Arungquiltha will help us.'

Polde got the ball of 'possum fur, and found that by using it very carefully, there would be just enough to make the eight strings that they needed, being four for each sandal.

'Let me pull some hair out to make your last shoe stronger,' said Polde, when she saw that Iliapa had finished the first of her own sandals. She took a wisp of her hair as she spoke, and tugged at it until she gave a little squeal, as at last she pulled out more than a hundred hairs.

At that moment, they heard a sound, as of some one walking overhead. They held their breaths, listening, and Iliapa at once put the stone into its place. Then there was complete silence.

'He has wakened up, and he is walking about,' said Iliapa. She knew it was a dangerous thing to do. But she was so bent on finishing her work that she once more took out the stone. The eagerness of her haste made her hands tremble. But the sun was getting low, and she knew that if she did not use the light now, in a short time it would be too late. Her hands steadied as she worked; she finished this last sandal in a much shorter time than any of the rest.

When the 'possum fur strings were fastened to the last sandal, the sun had gone down, and so little light came in through the opening, that this part of the work was done more by feeling than by sight. When Iliapa put the stone back in its place, a feeling of faintness came over her, that forced her to lie down.

'You have drunk only a little water, and you have hardly eaten a bit to-day. If you do not want to die in this cave, in place of getting to your boy, you had better eat and drink this minute,' said Polde, bringing the water-bag to Iliapa. They ate and drank together in the darkness, emptying the bag to the last drop, and eating what was left of the swan to the last bite. Then Iliapa at once fell fast asleep, and Polde kept watch to see what would come to pass.

CHAPTER 21

Iliapa had been asleep for a little more than two hours, when she was awakened by Polde pushing her, and softly calling her by name, saying:

'The two men that were away have come back, and they are talking fast. Listen, you can hear better than I do.'

They both crept close to the opening, where, through the crevices, the sounds came in distinctly. But the men were talking in a loud excited way, so that for a short time, Iliapa could only hear confused voices. At last she caught these words:

'They must be hiding somewhere near this hill; we are sure now that they have gone no further. We have searched all round for two miles. Whichever way they went, there is some sand that they would have to cross. We must have seen some tracks if they had gone on. Perhaps they have gone back on their tracks, and hidden in that piece of thick scrub, northward; or even crept into some hole in the ground.'

'Then they are hiding till they see us go away,' said the man who had been left to keep watch, and who had slept so soundly. 'While you were away,' he went on, 'I kept watch like an eagle-hawk. Once I thought I heard a talking, in the valley of the White Stone Creek, to the south, among those thick bushes, where we found the Arungquiltha.'

'Did you go and look where you heard the sound?' asked one.

'No, I knew if they were there, and came out, I must see them. It was wiser to stay where I could see the country all round. Now that you have killed a sheep, we can stay for another sun. But no longer, for our women will have no food, and they do not know how to work magic like these strange creatures.'

After this, there was no more talk; for the men had left the sheep at the foot of the hill, and they had now decided that it would be better to carry it up to the top, where they could get a clear space, on the rocks, for cooking, also they could keep up their watch. One made a big fire by the large flat stone, that covered the entrance to the cave, while the other two prepared the sheep for being cooked. They worked in silence, for they were very hungry, having had nothing to eat for more than twenty-four hours.

Iliapa and Polde knew nothing of what was going on, until dense smoke began to creep in through the cracks between the stones. For a moment or two they thought it was all up with them, that the Rock-Pigeon Men had in some way found out they were in the cave, and were now going to burn them out.

'Oh, it will be better to let them kill us, than to be roasted alive,' gasped Polde.

'Let us keep still, no flame has come near us yet. Don't make a noise, even if you choke,' whispered Iliapa. Polde found it hard to follow this advice, for the smoke was very sharp, and went up her nose and into her eyes, and down her throat, so that at the last she could not keep back some queer muffled sounds.

'Keep your mouth shut, and hold your hands tight over your eyes and ears,' said Iliapa, pressing her hands over Polde's eyes, and then placing her thumbs on her ears. Polde carried out this lesson and for some minutes there was not a sound to be heard.

Presently the smoke grew less, and the cave was filled with the smell of wool singed by fire.

'They are cooking the sheep, that is why they have made the big fire,' whispered Iliapa.

'Ah, how good it smells,' said Polde, sniffing up the air with delight. For the smell of singed wool soon gave place to that of roasting flesh. Iliapa sat perfectly still, without a word or a sign to show that she was alive.

'Oh, Iliapa, push my foot or make some sign to show you are not dead,' said Polde, at last, in a tearful whisper.

In an equally low tone, Iliapa replied:

'I am not dead, I am thinking. Listen, Polde. These Rock-Pigeon Men are very hungry; they will eat and eat until they can hold no more. After they have eaten, they will go to sleep. As soon as they have gone to sleep, then we must run for our lives, away to the White Stone Water-hole. It may be that they will come after us, but I do not believe they will catch us. Our only chance is to get away. Tie on your kuditcha shoes at once; let us be ready at the first moment that they fall asleep. When we go to the south, there is only a little strip of sand to cross. The shoes will last us over that bit.'

With shaking hands Polde tied on the shoes. Iliapa did the same. They waited in the darkness for what seemed to them long hours, before the last sound of talking died away. When at last no voice or sound reached them, Iliapa removed the side stone of the opening, and thrust out her head. It was a clear, warm night, the sky brilliant with stars. The moon was now late in rising, being on the wane.

For the first moment or two, Iliapa could make out nothing but the great wide heavens above, full of the soft star-light, and the earth below, dark and silent as if fast asleep, with no sound or sign of living creature. But as her eyes got used to the change from the deep gloom of the cave, she saw that one of the men was lying full length only a few yards away from the opening. His face was towards it, his spear, boomerang and shield beside him.

When first Iliapa saw his face plainly, the blood seemed to freeze in her veins with terror. His eyes were half open, so that he looked as if he were staring at her so hard, that he did not move an eyelash. She turned dizzy and sightless. But only for a few seconds. She saw by his deep regular breathing, and then by the sightless look of his eyes, that he was really sound alseep, that he was one of those people who sleep with eyes half open.

When she looked at the ground more closely, she could see the feet of another man, who was lying out of her range of sight, with his head towards the north. Of the third man she could see nothing. Could it be that he was keeping watch? Perhaps sitting on the great smooth stone from which he could see all round the hill?

'What do you see, Iliapa?' whispered Polde, who had crept to her side, and who had waited full of fear and wonder, while Iliapa stood with her head thrust out through the opening.

She now drew back, and putting the stone in its place, briefly told Polde what she had seen. The great question now was, should they steal out of the cave, without waiting any longer? They had not a drop of water, or a morsel of food, and if they were without food and water and fresh air for twenty-four hours longer, they would be too weak to make a long rapid stage to the White Stone Water-hole.

'If we could only be sure that the third man, you did not see, is fast asleep,' said Polde.

'Let me first go out alone to see,' said Iliapa.

'But if he is keeping watch and sees you, it is all the same as if he saw the two of us,' replied Polde. 'I think I should die, to be left here all alone.'

'No, you would not die. You would not even be as much afraid as I was when I thought the Rock-Pigeon Man, who sleeps with his eyes half open, was staring at me wide awake,' answered Iliapa. 'The more I think of it, the more I see that it would be better for me to take a look round before we both go out. For one thing, I can slip back in one moment if he is keeping watch. It would take twice as long for two to slip back. If he is keeping watch, he is looking out far, not under his very nose.'

'Still if you go under his very nose, he cannot help seeing you,' said Polde. 'But if he is sitting on the big smooth stone, you could easily see him without his seeing you.'

'Yes, and if he is further away, it would be still easier for me to see him, without being seen,' replied Iliapa. 'Now, Polde, whatever happens, keep quite quiet. If I have to stay a little longer than we expect, don't come out. If you hear sounds that you do not understand, don't come out. If. . . . '

'Whatever you say, Iliapa, you cannot turn me into a stone,' said Polde. 'If the Rock-Pigeon Men come to put out my eyes with a fire-stick, you may be quite sure that I will scream, no matter what you say to me beforehand.'

'If the men see me, and if they come to kill you, or to put out your eyes with a fire-stick, then all is over,' said Iliapa, 'and whether you scream out, or keep quiet as a snake in the grass, does not matter a leaf of salt-bush. But the thing is to be wise and quiet and careful, as long as one small chance is left to us of getting away. Here, keep my shoes for me; they will only last about an hour at the most. It is no use wearing them here.'

Iliapa stooped to untie her shoes. While she was doing this, a curious half-smothered sound fell on her ears. She at once sat up, saying in a whisper to Polde: 'Did you hear that? What is it?'

'Yes,' sobbed Polde, 'I heard that – I can tell you what it is. It is me crying my eyes out, because you are going to leave me here in the fearful darkness all alone. It is not much I ask of you. I say to you, "After coming all this way with you – after starving with hunger, and dying with thirst – after hearing my inside beat out loud over and over again, from fear of the Men of the Rock-Pigeon, who want to dash out our brains, and put out our eyes with burning fire-sticks – let me die with you. Do not let me die by myself like a rabbit that has eaten arsenic, in a hole all alone."

Polde, having kept back her tears while she spoke, now sobbed silently in a heart-broken way. Iliapa, too, began to cry – not sobbing, but with the tears rolling quickly down her cheeks.

'Polde, listen to me, and I will speak as if we were both going to die this moment,' she said, keeping her voice steady, so that Polde's courage might come back to her. 'If it was only you and me – if I had no boy, who lies awake and cries for me, then I would say to you: "Let us rush out together." If we die, we die. If we do not die, we get away. But because of my boy – because of Alibaka, who has no one in the whole world to care for him but me, and his father who is too far away to help, this is what I say to you, "Let us not run one risk that we can help. Let us tread as softly as if we were going over broken glass." If the third man is keeping watch, then we must wait. It may be that to-morrow, they will say one to the other, "These two women are cursed – there is some evil spirit who is helping them. We must get away for fear some foul thing comes to us." Then we can creep out. Though we may be weak, we can go slowly. Though we may be faint with hunger, we will get some small thing that crawls or flies. Though we may be parched with thirst, we will find some water-hole where there is a little bit of mud, or a secret well that is not quite dry. Then we will dig and dig, and the water will slowly rise. We shall eat and keep alive, we shall drink and get stronger. We shall crawl a little further on the way, and help will come to us. We shall meet the Afghans for whom we have a message, to give us help. At last the day will dawn when you will say, "What are these smokes that are rising up against the sky, like tall blue feathers?" And, Polde, one thing more. I believe with all my heart the Arungquiltha will help us. When I think how my father brought down rain from the sky, my fears go away.'

'Iliapa, let it be as you wish. You are wiser than I am. Go then, and look if you can see the third man, and I will stay alone, because if he is awake and watching, one can slip back into the cave quicker than two. Only stay a little longer with me, for it is as though we might never speak to each other again.'

Iliapa put her arm round Polde, and they sat close to each other for a few minutes, without saying a word. Then Iliapa arose, and said, 'You will see me coming back in a few minutes with good news.'

She removed the three stones, one by one. Before going out, she asked Polde to stand by the opening, while she looked round. The man who was so close, had turned over and now lay facing the other way, so that his face was hidden from view. But it was clear he was still fast asleep. Iliapa, on going outside, did not at once stand up. The second man, whose feet she could see before she came outside, was snoring loudly. She peered from side to side, trying to find out if the third man was in sight.

One quick glance showed her that he was not keeping watch on the stone above them. When she saw this, she stood upright, and looked anxiously all round. Then she saw a dark form standing up, leaning against a desert oak, that was about one hundred yards away, on the side furthest from the opening. While she was still watching him, this man strolled off in a northern direction.

Even as she watched him, Iliapa saw that the light which comes into the sky, before the day breaks, was spreading far and near. Many thoughts went quickly through her mind. But the chief one was, 'Now or never is the moment to get away.'

She turned her face towards the opening. Polde stood there holding the shoes in one hand, the other things in a heap near, all ready to be handed out.

'Come this moment,' she whispered. She tied on her shoes, took hold of her netted bag, and the two light blankets, leaving the empty water-bag, and the other things for Polde.

Just as Polde was stepping out, the man who lay close to the opening moved, and muttered something in his sleep. She almost dropped what she was carrying but kept hold of them, and stood as if rooted to the ground. Iliapa had gone some few paces before she found that Polde was not following. When she turned round to see where she was, she saw that the man who was awake had turned from the north, and was slowly walking towards the cave. This seemed to be the end. But when he came back to the desert oak, against which he had been leaning before, he stood still for a moment or two, and then lay down, stretching himself at full length on the ground.

At the same moment Polde joined Iliapa, who said to her in a whisper, 'Now let us run for our lives.'

They crept away down the sloping side until they got to the foot of the hill; then they went at their utmost speed, and the dawn was spreading in the east, as red as flames of fire, when they reached the strip of sand that they had to cross, before turning full south, and following the White Stone Creek.

CHAPTER 22

Once they had crossed the strip of sand, they untied the shoes, and buried them under the branches of a fallen tree. They got on much faster after this, for the grass and feathers, though tightly bound together with hair, had been coming to pieces. They had, however, served the purpose, that in crossing the sand no toe- or foot-mark had been made – only a dim impression that bore no likeness to a human foot. They had also taken care to keep at some distance from each other, so as to make these marks look more accidental.

The country as they went on opened out into a fine well-wooded plain; in places there was tall grass that the sun had dried and bleached almost to perfect whiteness. But there was no spinifex, nor prickly bushes, nor stones, nor dead wood, so that they got on very quickly. They did not stop, nor speak a word, except when, now and then, one of them would cast a hasty look behind, and say to the other, 'No one.'

As the sun mounted in the sky they both suffered dreadfully from thirst. They were, in fact, getting so weak and spent, that they felt if they once sat down they could hardly go on again. So, except for a few pauses, they did not stop until about an hour before mid-day, when the gleam of white stones was to be seen through the dark green of the mulga-trees.

'Can it be the White Stone Water-hole?' said Iliapa. It seemed too good to be true, for it was more than hour sooner than they had hoped to get there. But though they had been so much worn down by hunger, and fear, and thirst, and want of sleep, they had walked more quickly for a longer stretch of time than they had ever walked before.

The thought that never left Iliapa's mind was 'If the Rock-Pigeon Men catch up to us, I shall never, never see my boy again. He will cry for me in the night and there will be no one to care for him.' The thought that kept hammering in Polde's brain was: 'If we do not get away from the Rock-Pigeon Men, they will put out our eyes with fire-sticks, and leave us to die, blind and helpless, like the woman of the Plum-tree People, who stole a girdle of hair that belonged to the Men of Long-Ago.'

So the great love of a mother for her child, and the great fear that a young strong woman has of death, had kept them up, and urged them on, until now at last, at last, they reached this place of refuge, where they could get food and water, and stay to bathe and rest.

The banks round the water-hole were high and steep, except on the northern side, where the bed of the White Stone Creek came into it. On this side, then, Iliapa and Polde went to the water. One might say that they stumbled rather than walked, the last hundred yards or so. Their legs were trembling violently, and their backs ached so acutely that it was hard for them to keep from falling down.

But the water was deep and clear, and in the shade of the mulga-trees, still cool. After drinking one pannikinful after the other, they bathed at the sunny end of the water-hole, where the water was perfectly warm, just as if it had been poured out of a kettle that had been some time on the fire. Polde dived deep, time after time, like a duck, but Iliapa contented herself with swimming from side to side, and around about. Afterwards the two lay down in the shade. Oh, how good it was to hear the birds, and rest without fear of a cruel death! There were the sharp cries of cockatooes, and the shrieking of parrots, mingled with the soft cooing notes of pigeons; the low flat cries of ducks, and now and again the harsh croaking of a bittern. It all seemed to Iliapa like the low crooning songs her mother used to sing long, long ago. Like the songs she herself had chanted to Alibaka, when he was a small baby, and fell asleep against her heart. Her last thought was: 'I shall see him, I shall see him, when a few more suns have come and gone.'

When she awoke the sun was low in the west, and Polde had been about for some time. She had not been idle, for she had snared two ducks among the reeds that grew thick at the northern end of the pool, and was making a fire on which to cook them.

'Polde, you are very clever to snare wild-fowl as you do,' said Iliapa cheerfully. 'I am sure that if I tried to do it, the only thing that I should do would be to frighten them all away.'

After they had cooked and eaten these, they felt so much refreshed and rested, they thought it was better to go on a stage before camping for the night.

They had now cast away all fear of the Rock-Pigeon Men. But they had lost a great deal of time; and they now thought of Hussein's caravan. Well, even if they missed him, they could still pull through. Getting away from the fear of torture and death, made other trials seem small.

'And they are often kept for two or three suns on the way,' said Polde. 'They do not come by the White Stone Water-hole; they go to a station on the east, a whole sun off the straight road. If we go on to-night we have more chance of meeting them.'

So they went on, and a good thing it was that they did so. They camped for the night by a native well, which was within sight of the Overland Telegraph Line. Next morning they were up and on their way before the sun rose. When it was about two hours high in the sky, they saw a cloud of dust far away ahead of them.

'Can it be another storm of sand?' said Polde, taking a tighter hold of her things as she looked. She did not want to be whirled off and half buried a second time. But Iliapa reminded her that even if there was a storm, there was no desert of sand.

'It is Hussein', she said, after going on for another quarter of an hour. And sure enough it was. In the clear light of the morning, while yet a long way off, they could see the file of camels, one after the other, with their long legs and long curved necks, and the even steady strides with which they got over the ground.

After the yearly sheep-shearing, when the wool is taken from the stations to the railhead, the loading of the camels is a simple affair, a bale of wool being fastened to each side of their pack-saddles. But the loads they carried to the stations are very different. They are composed not only of provisions and domestic utensils, but often comprise such items as water-tanks, great buckets used in well-sinking, sheets of galvanized iron, lengths of sawn timber, deal doors, window-frames, etc., etc. The outline of such cargoes are fantastic, yet eloquent of the far-flung settlements of our race; suggestive, too, of the way in which the kingdoms of the world have been formed from time immemorial – men pushing out into unpeopled regions, bearing with them stores and implements, and the rude beginnings of a home.

'What if it should not be Hussein after all,' said Iliapa, pausing as they drew near the caravan. The last few days had shaken her a good deal, and made her feel timid and fearful of new dangers. But while she was yet speaking, an Afghan came forward, in advance of his companions and the file of camels. He waved his hand and called out: 'Balkara.' He had got a message from Antaka, at a telegraph station on the way, which the telegraph master had explained to him, so that he knew who the two women were as soon as he caught sight of them, and before Iliapa had given him the message that she had kept so carefully in her netted bag. He had been expecting to meet them, before he left the telegraph line. An hour later, he had to turn due east, to deliver some goods at a station caled Ultamba. So that if the travellers had camped all night at the White Stone Water-hole, they could not have met him at all.

He gave them as much food as would last them till they got to Ergume, the telegraph station, at which they were to stay and rest for a day, as the people there now knew about them and wished to be kind to them. When they left Erguma, it would take them little more than a week to get to Labalama.

That night they both felt so happy that they sang corrobboree chants, and Polde told tales of the Great One, and the Blue Dove; and, last of all, stories of the children of Moorano, who had cupboards full of tales and pictures of the 'Good little Queen of England and of the Blacks.'

CHAPTER 23

Next morning they went on their way just as the sun rose.

In about an hour they reached a beautiful park-like plain, covered with tall white grass, having groups of lovely trees scattered over it, chiefly box and gum. The sight of this plain made Polde begin to sing her favourite chant, with new flourishes inspired by a joyful sense of victory:

'Oh, what is this I see? Smoke and smoke and smoke. Not passing soon away, like the brush fire of a mia-mia. No, smoke that stays, and goes on curling up into the sky, like the great blue feathers of a kingfisher, that has turned into an emu. Whose smoke can this be? Is it the fire of Afghans, carrying strange things for white men? No – for they make but one or two fires, and here there are many. Grey dove, singing in the trees, tell me, for you know – whose fires are these that smoke blue, blue as the skies of the morning? Listen, listen, and hear the dove say, "The smokes you see, are the smokes of Labalama, of Labalama – ama – ama."'

When she had sung so long that she did not care to sing any longer, Polde stopped and turned round, expecting to see Iliapa smiling with her eyes, her mouth and cheeks. But instead of that, what did she see? She saw Iliapa with her head bent, her sun-bonnet pulled well over her face, like a woman who has a sorrow that she wants to hide from other eyes.

'You are very strange,' said Polde in a vexed tone.

'No, I am not strange, only afraid; as we get nearer, the fear sometimes grows bigger. What if Alibaka is not there? What if Simon has taken him away to a place unknown to me? What if. . . . '

'I will tell you another thing, too,' said Polde, stopping her, 'what if the moon turned into a big boomerang, and came down and struck him on the head, and then flew back into the sky again?' As at other times, she went on making up still more absurd accidents, until at last Iliapa fairly laughed. Then Polde was pleased, and they both began to make plans for the day that they should get to Labalama.

The fine well-wooded country came to an end two hours before sunset. They had got on so fast that they camped by a creek, without going any further.

Late on in the evening, some days after this, they reached the telegraph station of Erguma. Here they were treated with very great kindness, and what delighted Iliapa still more, here she got some news of her boy. One of the clerks in the telegraph station had been at Labalama a few days before, and had seen a black boy who was called 'Baka,' riding a race-horse that belonged to Simon. When the clerk heard that this boy was Iliapa's, and that she was going there to get him back, he said to her: 'Is there any white person in the place who knows about you?' She showed him the letter in the little silk bag, and he told her that the doctor was the best man to help her, and advised her to go to him as soon as they reached Labalama, before she saw Simon, or told anyone else why they had come, or even tried to see her boy.

At Ergume telegraph station, they were given as much bread and meat, tea and sugar and biscuits as would last them to Labalama. The kind white Missus made them stay for a day, and some of the black women who were there helped the two to wash their clothes and sun-bonnets. When they were ironed out they looked almost as if they were new.

At the end of the eighth day, after leaving Erguma, Polde climbed into a gum-tree. 'What do I see?' she began to chant. Iliapa at first would not believe that Polde saw the smokes of Labalama. She thought that it was still a good many miles away, and that if Polde really saw any smoke, it was not the smoke from houses in the township.

'Then come on a little further and see for yourself,' said Polde. So they went on a little further, and at the end of half an hour, they saw three smokes curling up quite blue and steady into the sky. In ten minutes more they saw several tents. Then they knew it was the camp of some white men, and that they were still some miles away from Labalama.

They did not go near the tents, but kept well out of sight, walking among the trees that grew along a wide creek, that was called Jerama, in the Arunta tongue. The word means 'To roast,' and it had been given that name because the creek is so good for game.

Polde knew that this creek was about an hour's walk away from the township. The night had now closed in; there was a high north-east wind blowing, and the sky was so full of clouds that no stars were to be seen. 'Shall we camp here for the night, and get into Labalama early in the morning?' asked Polde as they stopped to rest by a pool of water in the Jerama.

It was some little time before Iliapa could make up her mind as to what would be the wisest thing to do. She knew from what Polde said that there were always some blacks in the township, and that the moment they met any of these, they would have more questions asked than she could count. 'Where did you come from?' 'Are you all alone?' 'Why did you come?' 'Are you going to stay here long?'

Well, she would know how to put off any questions that she did not wish to answer. But then there would be sure to be some at Labalama who would know Polde. At once the report would be spread, from one to the other. 'You know that boy who rides the race-horses so well for Simon? Well, his mother has come all the way from the middle of the Country of the Salt Water. She is here, she is with Polde, whose man died here many moons ago.'

So the news might come to Simon, before she had ever set eyes on her boy. And what would Simon do then? Why, he might call to Alibaka and say, 'Put the saddles on two of my fast horses, as quick as ever you can – we have to go far away at once.' And Alibaka would obey, not knowing that his mother was quite near – not knowing that she was as a creature who is starving to hold him once more in her arms. And he would ride away to some place quite unknown to her. At the thought a great sob arose in her throat.

'Are you crying because you are so near your boy?' asked Polde, half laughing, half angry.

'No, no – not because I am so near him, but because though he might be so close to me, that I could throw a stone where he stood, yet I may not set eyes on him,' cried Iliapa, quite unable to keep back her tears, though she knew very well that she would seem to Polde like a creature that has lost her reason. Then she grew calm, and said in a firm voice: 'Yes, let us camp here to-night. It will be wiser, for then I go to the doctor's house before he is up – before any of our people are about or can see us. After I see him, we will ask for Nabata.'

They kindled a fire, but quite a small one, low in a branch of the Jerama, where it was dry, so that it would not be seen by anyone who might be coming that way. As soon as they made some tea, they put the fire out. After they had lain down close to each other in a sheltered spot, Polde suddenly started up.

'What is that I hear, like footsteps quite near us?' she whispered.

'It is not footsteps – it is my heart – it beats so hard as if it were up in my ears – I cannot make it be still, for I am thinking all the time that Alibaka is so near me to-night,' said Iliapa.

CHAPTER 24

Iliapa slept very little that night. When she did fall asleep, she would soon start awake again, and look to see if the dawn was breaking. When at last she saw a brightness coming into the east and heard some magpies beginning to sing, she said to herself, 'Is this the day when I shall see my boy once more?' She could hardly believe it.

She got up and saw that it really was a new day. She lit a fire and made some tea, and then awoke Polde, who got up with her eyes still full of sleep.

'Are we quite near Labalama, or have I been dreaming foolish dreams?' she said, rubbing her eyes.

'You have not been dreaming foolish dreams, for we are quite near the place,' replied Iliapa. She could not keep her voice steady. Indeed, it was very hard for her to keep from crying. So she did not say another word, until Labalama lay in full view.

There was no smoke, however, arising from any of the houses, for the sun was not up yet, and no one was stirring. Iliapa kept on staring ahead, and from side to side, for she thought: 'At any moment I might see Alibaka – perhaps riding one of the fast horses.'

Then, too, she thought of her sister, Nabata, and wondered if she was in the township, or away in the camp at some distance. Would she see her first, before she saw Alibaka; and had Nabata found out that he was her sister's boy? It was so very long ago since that morning she woke up to find that Nabata was gone.

Close to the northern outskirts of the township, they saw some mia-mias with a little smoke curling up in front of one of them. They stood for a time looking at these mia-mias, wondering whether it would be better for them, after all, to go straight there, and ask where the doctor lived.

'We could tell them we had come a long way, and that before we do anything else, we have to give a letter to the doctor. That would make them think we have been sent from some white people,' said Polde.

'But there might be some one who would know – some one who would tell Simon before I see Alibaka,' replied Iliapa. 'When we get into the township, there is sure to be some one to show us the doctor's house.'

So they kept away to the left, out of sight of the mia-mias, and this brought them close up to the railway station. There were two men beginning to work, unloading some goods from a truck. Iliapa took the letter out of the little silk bag, and went up to one of the men. She showed him the letter and asked him to tell her where the doctor lived.

'Do you see the pepper-trees over in front of that house?' he said, pointing to one that was about a quarter of a mile away from the railway station. 'That is where the doctor lives; there are two of them there just now, for the old doctor has had an accident.'

Iliapa was so excited that she did not take in what he meant. When they got to the house, they went round to the back-door, and knocked. They were kept waiting for some time, and when the door was opened, it was by a Chinaman, who spoke English much more brokenly than Iliapa did. She showed him the letter, and asked if she could see the doctor. The Chinaman said the doctor was not about yet, but would be up in a quarter of an hour. He told them to wait, and they sat down in the veranda at the back of the house.

'What a long time he is coming,' said Polde after a few minutes, giving a great yawn as she spoke. It was so dull waiting like this with Iliapa as silent as if she had been turned into a stick or a stone. She longed to go to the camp of the other natives, to talk and laugh – perhaps to cry a little, as she heard of all that had taken place since she was at Labalama.

But at last the door was opened, and the doctor came out. Iliapa sprang up eagerly, and held out the letter to him. He took it and looked at the address.

'This is not for me,' he said, 'this is for Dr Grey, who is in bed too ill to read a letter, or even to speak. Perhaps I had better open it for him.'

'The Missus of Antaka said I must give it only to Dr Grey,' said Iliapa. The tears had come into her eyes and she was trembling a little. It was a fearful disappointment to her, that this was not the doctor who was Mrs Browne's friend, and who would be sure to do all he could for her. In her confusion, she could only feel that she must keep to what she had been told – to give the letter only to Dr Grey.

'Is it about some one who is ill?' asked the young doctor, who was touched by the pitiful look in Iliapa's face.

At this moment Polde began to sob aloud, and then Iliapa could no longer keep back her tears. They rolled silently down her cheeks while she held the letter, that the doctor had given back to her, and told him it was not about anyone who was ill.

There came a loud knock at the front door, the Chinaman came to tell the doctor that he was wanted at the Emu Inn, where some one had been taken very ill.

'Wait here till I come back – perhaps there may be something I can do for you,' said the doctor, looking from Iliapa to Polde. As he went away, he ordered the Chinaman, Ching Moon, who was cook and general servant in the house, to give the two strange black women a good meal. He did so, and shortly after Iliapa fell fast asleep.

Polde, who had slept well all night, and was not at all tired, now felt very lonely. She sat for a time quite still, while Iliapa slept. At last she felt that she must go and look about her – just take a short walk, to see what was going on. It was nice and lively to be in town, after such a long, dreary, tiring journey.

She stole away, and strolled towards the post office and telegraph station. She wondered who the people were who lived there now, and whether they had children, and a black girl or lubra. She did not mean to go close to the place, but one thing after another drew her on.

First, there was a train going out, and the long line of carriages, that went so quickly without horses or camels, and just thick black smoke puffing out of a narrow chimney, always seemed to Polde a wonderful thing. She walked on quickly, watching it as far as she could see it. When it went out of sight, she was close to the railway yard, and in this there were a number of camels, and some Afghans, who like Hussein were going to take goods to stations far and near. The goods were arranged in heaps, so much for each. Then the camels were made to kneel down, while the goods, tightly corded together, were fixed on the saddle – an equal weight on each side. Two of the camels were rather wild, and refused to lie down, trying to kick and bite the men who were attending to them.

Polde was so much interested in all that was going on – she quite forgot she was in the busiest part of the township, and might at any moment be seen by some one who would know her. And this was what took place.

'Polde, Polde – where have you come from?' cried some one close beside her. Polde turned with a start from looking into the railway yard, and was delighted to see Membata, the greatest friend she had when she lived at Labalama. They laughed till the tears ran down their cheeks, and each talked at the top of her voice, asking questions of the other without waiting for a reply.

When they got a little quieter, Membata again asked: 'But where have you come from?'

Polde now wished she had stayed with Iliapa or kept away where she would not meet any of her old friends, for she had little skill in refusing to tell what she knew. But she made a brave effort.

'Look here now – by-and-by I will tell you a fine long story – now I only tell you I come a long, long way – from the far side of the Red Sand Desert.'

'But that is many, and many, and many a sun from here. Why did you come so far, and who was with you?'

Polde lost her head, and could not think what to say.

'I came – I came with Iliapa,' she said; 'But do not ask me why we came.'

'Iliapa? Iliapa, the daughter of the medicine man, Erungara? Then you need not tell me why you have come. It is after her boy Alibaka. You know he is here, and her sister Nabata as well.'

'Memba, Memba,' cried a little fair-haired girl, running up to Membata. 'What in the world is keeping you? Mother is waiting for you all this time.'

Membata, who was carrying some parcels from a small general store, that was on the opposite side of the railway station, at once ran off with the little girl, crying out to Polde as she went, 'See you again soon.'

'What will Iliapa say? I ought not to have told her,' thought Polde. But somehow she could not be very sorry. For had she not heard a most exciting piece of news – that Alibaka was really here, that he had not been taken away by Simon to some unknown place, as Iliapa had sometimes feared.

Polde ran nearly all the way back to the doctor's house. Iliapa was awake, and very much astonished to find that Polde had gone away. She had asked Ching Moon if she knew where she was, but he only his head and said, 'No, sabe.'

'I have been to the railway station. . . . ' began Polde, almost breathless with running.

'Oh, Polde – were you not afraid that some one would see you?' cried Iliapa reproachfully.

'Some one did see me – my old mate Membata. And what a good thing it was I saw her; for she told me that your boy is here, also your sister Nabata.'

'Is he really here? Oh, where, where – did she tell you the house?' cried Iliapa, forgetting everything else in her joy.

Polde told how Membata had been called away, while she was still talking, by a little girl.

'Did you see what house she went to?' asked Iliapa. No, Polde had not thought of that.

'And did you not tell her not to let anyone know that I am here? Oh, some trouble will come upon us yet – Simon will hear, and will carry off my boy before I can even look at him,' cried Iliapa, her old fears crowding back on her.

She began putting her things together, as if she was going somewhere, but she really hardly knew what she was doing. The unlooked-for illness of the good doctor, who would have been her friend, filled her with confusion. If she had been able to reason better, she would have known that her best plan was to let the young man who was acting for Dr Grey open the letter. But she could only think that Mrs Browne had warned her: 'Be sure you do not give the letter to anyone but Dr Grey. If you trust it to anyone else it may get lost.'

'Then because the old medicine man is ill, must we get into a hole, and hide like two wombats?' asked Polde with some anger. 'For more days than we can count, we have been in sand and lonely places, where there were no trees, or grass or water. We have been nearly dead with hunger and thirst; we have been nearly killed, and had our eyes put out with fire-sticks. Now we have come to the place where your boy is alive and well, where your sister is, who was always good to you; where big carriages go fast on wheels, without a horse or camel near them; where people walk about all day, and talk and laugh; where camels go on their knees as if they were at a Mission Station. Are you going to be afraid all the time and make a hole to hide in every day?'

Polde stopped because she was out of breath. Iliapa, who had listened carefully to every word she said, was silent for a little, turning things over in her mind. Then she said:

'You are right, Polde. It is no use trying to hide now that we are at Labalama. Let us come and see if we can find your mate Membata. When she shows me where Alibaka lives, I will go and say in sight of all men: "This is my boy, he belongs to me; he was stolen from me." Then we will go and find Nabata.'

They gathered up their things and went away, not even remembering that the young doctor had asked them to wait till he came back. But as they were going out of the gate in front, Ching Moon came out, and told them that the doctor had been called to a place twenty miles from the township, and would not be back till late in the evening.

They went towards the railway station, as they both thought that the house to which Membata had been called by the little girl might not be far off. This turned out to be right, for in front of a small iron house, a little way to the left of the station, they saw a child with fair hair standing by a baby go-cart, and before they got up to her, Membata came out of the house with a baby in her arms.

She gave a little cry of delight on seeing Polde and Iliapa, and putting the child in the go-cart, she asked them to walk with her to the general store on the other side of the railway station.

'Your sister, Nabata, works at the Emu Inn,' she said to Iliapa; 'she comes down from the camp every day, and goes back at night.'

'And my boy, Alibaka – do you know where he lives?' asked Iliapa. Membata was not quite sure, but thought that Simon stayed mostly at the Emu Inn. On hearing this, Iliapa said she would go there at once. Polde, of course, went with her.

CHAPTER 25

The Emu Inn was a big irregular building that had straggled into about twenty-two rooms, by having some added from time to time as they were needed. When Iliapa and Polde got there, they saw a great many people standing round the front doors.

'Hello, you two – are you strangers here; where did you come from?' cried some one as they passed, Iliapa looked hard from one to the other, thinking all the time that at any moment she might see her boy. When the man spoke, she nudged Polde in the side, saying in the Arunta tongue, 'Do not speak.'

'They don't know any English,' said the man. 'Yet where did they come from, togged up like white women?' This made Polde giggle, and Iliapa was glad when they got away from the front to the back of the inn, where there was a big yard, with stables and other outbuildings. There was a black man chopping wood, and a white woman washing up dishes on a table under the back veranda.

Iliapa went up to her at once and asked: 'Is Nabata here?'

'Yes, she is cleaning out the bedrooms,' replied the woman, staring at the new-comers with some surprise. 'She will soon come out if you wait.'

In a short time Nabata came out, with an armful of mats that she was going to shake.

'Nabata, do you know me?' said Iliapa, going up to her. It was twelve years since the sisters had seen each other. Nabata, who was twenty when they parted, was of course quite grown up at that time and still so much like her father, that the younger sister would have known her anywhere. But Nabata looked at Iliapa in silence, without once thinking that the tall woman she saw before her, with a grave anxious face, was the little girl whom she had so often carried on her back.

'What is your name, and where have you come from?' she asked at last.

'I am Iliapa – I have come from Balkara.'

Ah, then there were loud cries and laughing, and clinging to each other; questions without answers, and answers but half made, Polde joining in all the time, half laughing, half weeping, making more noise than anyone.

'Have you come for your boy?' said Nabata at last in a low voice.

'I have come for him,' said Iliapa in a whisper, for fear anyone might hear her. 'Where is he at this moment? Oh, I want to see him. It is as if I could not wait a moment longer.'

'All that is inside of us is shaking to see him,' said Polde, her voice trembling, the tears running down her cheeks.

'Wait till I finish my work – that will be but a little time,' said Nabata. 'Do you see where that little mia-mia is beside the fence; you go and sit down there, and then I will come with some dinner. The old woman who is there is my mother-in-law. If. . . . '

One called to Nabata from the kitchen, so she made haste to beat the mats against the fence of the yard, and then hurried inside. Iliapa and Polde went out by the slip-panel gate, and walked up towards the mia-mia, that was made of old cases, and some gum boughs with bags over them. There was a big trunk of a gum-tree not far from this, and here the two sat until Nabata and another woman came with dinner for all of them.

But before Iliapa could eat or drink, she heard all that her sister could tell her of Alibaka.

'He is better now,' said Nabata, 'but when he came here, he was thin and ill. Every day he wanted to get back to you. More than once he tried to run away, then Simon was cruel to him. It is only a few suns ago that I found out that he was the grandson of my father Erungara, and your boy. To-day they are at a little place where white men are looking for gold. When they come back in the evening, I will find Alibaka and tell him that you are here.'

'Show me the road to this little gold place,' cried Iliapa, starting up from the log on which she had been sitting, with the look of one who is about to run a race.

'But you are not going there now? It will be foolish of you, if you let Simon see you too soon,' said Nabata.

'No – no, I am not going there, but I want to wait where I cannot be seen, and watch for them to come back,' replied Iliapa.

Nabata made her come to eat some dinner, before going to sit and wait in this way. But it was not much that Iliapa could swallow just then. The nearer the time came when she might see her boy, the harder it was to wait.

Nabata showed her the track by which Simon would come from Yarana, as the little township was called. Close to this track, about half a mile from Labalama, there was a narrow gully full of straggling salt-bushes. Here it was easy to hide and still be quite close to the road, and see anyone that passed.

Here, then, Iliapa sat hour after hour with her eyes fixed on the track.

It was after sunset, when she saw a cloud of red dust rising up in the distance. A few minutes later, two riders came in sight, the one who rode foremost leading a horse. For a little time longer she could only see that there was another rider behind. But a few minutes later she saw that this rider was a black boy.

It was Alibaka.

'Oh, it is my boy – it is – it is,' she said to herself, over and over, hardly able to keep from calling out to him. Her heart was ticking like a strong clock, and her lips kept moving all the time. He passed so close to her, that if she had spoken above a whisper, he could at once have heard her. But she kept quite still, and only when her boy and Simon were getting into the township, did she rise up, and follow them as quickly as if she had wings on her heels.

She watched them riding up to the Emu Inn. Here Simon got off his horse and Alibaka led him round to the stables. Her first thought was to rush after him. But at that moment she saw Simon coming out of the inn with some other man. She sat down on the log near the mia-mia, where she could hear Polde laughing and talking without a pause.

Polde was indeed now in her true element – free from care and danger, with plenty to eat, and no end of news to hear and to tell from far and near. The people of the inn had told her that if she helped with the work of the house, they would be very glad to give her food, and an overall apron to keep her dress clean. She came to tell this to Iliapa, and when she heard that Alibaka was at that moment in the back yard near the stable, she could hardly contain herself.

'Oh, come to him at once,' she cried. 'What can Simon do to keep him from you? He is your boy. Or would you like me to go and say to

Alibaka that there is some one here who wants to speak to him?'

'Don't, don't – Simon is there. We must be careful or we might spoil everything,' said Iliapa. She held her head in her hands, feeling weak and a little giddy. To have seen her boy, without being able to rush to him, and hold him at last in her arms, was almost more than she could bear. But she had a great fear as to what Simon might do, to keep Alibaka from her – a fear so great that it made her silent and motionless till Polde lost all patience with her.

'Nabata knows and I know that Alibaka is your boy. Come now to Simon this moment and tell him loud and bold that you have come all the way from Balkara for your own boy, and that you must have him at once. Then I will speak, then also Nabata, and make this bad boy-stealing thief so much afraid – he will shake like a little girl when she sees a big poison snake.' Polde's voice rose by degrees till at last she was almost shouting.

'Keep still, Polde,' replied Iliapa in a low voice; 'we are only two black women. I have often heard my father say that many of the white people have been wicked and cruel to the blacks, and there has been no one to stand up for them and to say: "You must not do this." Black women and girls and boys have been stolen away, and when black men have gone to get them back, they have been shot down like wild dogs. That is why the Missus of Antaka wrote the letter. She knew that the doctor would help us, would stand up for us, and get me back my boy. Now the doctor is so ill – he cannot even speak. Nabata says I must take care, I must wait yet a little till my boy is alone.'

While they were speaking Nabata came from the inn, carrying a basket full of food. She knew that Simon and Alibaka had come, and as soon as she saw Iliapa, she said to her in a low voice, 'When Simon begins to play cards after his dinner, then I will bring Alibaka round to you here.'

They went to the mia-mia and had tea with the rest that were there. At any rate, Iliapa tried to, but it was little she could do in the way of eating. She was glad to drink some tea, for her throat was dry, and now and then she shivered a little though her head felt as hot as fire.

As soon as tea was over, Nabata went back to the inn. Iliapa went with her as far as the gum log, and there she sat waiting. It was a very warm, still night, without a breath of cool air. There was the sound of loud voices and laughing and singing at the inn, inside and out. A man was playing a concertina in the veranda, and while some men were singing the air he played, others were dancing.

Another was playing a piano, in a room with the windows and doors wide open, so that it seemed as if he played outside.

Iliapa listened to it all, but like one in a dream, where things happen as if a long way off. The sky was covered with clouds, not a star to be seen, and she was glad of this as she stood in the darkness with the lamps of the inn making a circle of light round the house. She stood staring at the lighted space, making sure that she would see Alibaka and Nabata when they came to her.

After waiting for some time, however, she heard whispering behind her.

'Yes, she came this morning.'

'Oh, Nabata, are you sure? Did you see her with your own eyes? Did you speak to her?'

It was the voice of Alibaka, and on hearing it, Iliapa gave a little low, stifled cry. The next moment he was in her arms – Alibaka, her own boy. At last, at last she held him close. It was as if she could never let him go. How many nights she had lain awake, and wept, fearing that she might never again set eyes on him. But here he was at last – alive and well.

It was some time before they could speak, and then there was so much to say that they could not keep to one thing long, but went on to something else. What filled Alibaka with endless wonder was, that his mother and Polde should have come all that way walking from Balkara, over such burning sand, such waste tracts of country, such waterless stretches, in which there were no beasts or birds for food. Even with good horses, such as Simon's, and with a few places to stop at on the way, where they could rest and get what they wanted, it had been a hard journey. Thinking of these things, Alibaka more than once put his arms round his mother, and said over and over again: 'Ah, how good you are, how good you are.' To Iliapa this was more than a reward for all she had gone through. When she felt the strong young arms of her boy round her, she cried with joy. They sat on the big gum log in the warm darkness, side by side, now talking, now silent. At times they began to say something and stopped short, saying, 'I forget what I was going to tell you.' Then in the middle of a sentence, the other would whisper: 'Ah, but I have you now – now all the long journey is over.' They spoke of Nalbuka, and said he, too, might soon be with them. The joy of finding each other once more seemed to bring this other happiness nearer.

'You have got so thin,' said Alibaka, after some moments of silence, clasping his mother's arms, which were indeed little more than skin and bone.

'And you have got taller – feel how high you reach,' said Iliapa, standing up and holding him against her side.

'Come into the light where I can see your face,' she added, leading the way through the slip-panel in the fence. They went near enough to the back of the inn to be within the circle of light that came through open doors and windows.

They stood looking into each other's faces, laughing in a happy way, no longer thinking of any danger that might still hang over them, and the risk they ran of being seen by Simon, or some one who would tell him that ''Baka's mother had come for him.' For by this time all the blacks that worked round the inn – and there were several, besides those that have been named – knew who the two strangers were, and why they had come.

'Now I must tell Polde to come and see you,' said Iliapa, running back to the gate. She softly called to Polde, who came to her crying out in a loud glad voice: 'Now, you see, you have got your boy – didn't I tell you true many and many a time?' They both went back to Alibaka, and Polde almost shouted for joy, to see what a fine, handsome, well-grown lad he was. 'Ah, if you had only seen us the time we were hiding from the Rock-Pigeon Men,' she cried.

Before Alibaka could say a word in reply, they heard heavy steps drawing near, and at the same moment they heard a harsh thick voice, saying, 'What are you doing here?'

It was Simon

CHAPTER 26

He was a short, thick man, with a face the colour of an old brick, red hair and beard, and small dark eyes that were swimming in fat. He looked very angry, as he glanced from one to the other of the three before him – from the mother to the son, and then at Polde, who was unwise enough to laugh in his face. This made him still more angry and he called again in a harsh voice, 'I ask you what are you doing talking with these strange blacks?'

'This is my mother, who has come all the way from Balkara for me,' said Alibaka proudly, resting his right hand on his mother's shoulder. She put her arm round his waist, drew him closer, and looking into Simon's face without a trace of fear, said:

'This is my own boy – my own Alibaka. Yukuta stole him from me. Now I have come for him – he is my own.'

'Upon my soul – talk of the cheek of white people – it's nothing to the cheek of niggers!' exclaimed Simon, adding several very ugly words, that were never long missing from his talk.

'Do you really mean to tell me,' he went on, looking hard at Iliapa with a furious scowl, 'that you think you are going to take this boy, this Alibaka away from me?'

'That is why I come all the long way,' replied Iliapa.

'This is my own mother: Yukuta had nothing to do with me. He told you lies,' said Alibaka, who could feel that his mother was trembling all over.

'You think we leave this boy with you, when we come flying aber him in the early day, and the late night?' said Polde, clenching her fists hard, as if she were getting ready to knock some one down. 'You big one fool, if you think um that.'

'But what business have you got to put your jaw into this? Who are you that you should be so cheeky, and speak when you are not spoken to?' snarled Simon, turning on Polde with a furious gesture.

But Polde was not easily cowed. She had before this seen black men quarrelling – and shrieking at each other till they were more hoarse than crows. She had known how to take her own part at such times, so that ugly words and loud angry talk, and threatening motions with the hands, made no more impression on her than water on a duck's back.

'What business?' she cried, echoing Simon's words. 'A lot of business. Iliapa my mate – her boy, my boy too. We come for him; we get him. What for you steal him, like wild cat tooken away little chickum?'

'Do you dare to say I stole him? roared Simon. 'Do you know I could have you put in jail for telling a lie like that?'

'Put me in jail,' said Polde with a loud laugh. 'No, no, no; this good dear boy was stealed from Balkara; now he is in Labalama – who branged him? You no steal him? All right; he come with his mother – he come with me – he belong to his mother – he belong to me – you no got nosing to do wif him. Have you ever hear of the Queen Ickoria, the bestest little Queen of Inglan' an' of the Blacks? My word – she break the cocoa-nut of anyone that stoled a black boy from his mother.'

'If you think you are going to get away this boy with a yarn like that, you are a fool for your pains,' said Simon, turning his back on Polde and facing Iliapa, but speaking in a lower voice, for the loud talking had by this time drawn people from the inn who came asking, 'What all the row was about.'

'There's no row,' replied Simon. 'It's just a couple of nigger women who are trying to play a joke on me. This one,' pointing to Polde as he spoke, 'is likely to get into trouble, if she does not take care to keep a quiet tongue in her head. She seems to me to be a lunatic that has run away from some asylum.'

Polde, in common with all Australian natives, got angry if anyone pointed at her.

'And you,' she said, pointing in turn at Simon, 'you will get into troubles more bad, if you no take care. I tell you plain, if the good Queen of Inglan' an' of the Blacks knowed you stoled a boy away from his mother, she would jolly soon put you in jail with han'-cuffs on, to keep you from any ozer stealing. Yes – an' if you don't take care – the good Queen of Inglan' an' of the Blacks – she have your head chop' off like one small fly.'

'Oh, Polde, don't say any more to him,' whispered Iliapa, who could see that this second attack made Simon almost speechless with rage. But the men who were listening laughed and clapped their hands.

'It's true as daylight,' said the cook, a large stout woman, who had come out to see if she could get a breath of fresh air, and stood listening to what was said, first by one and then by the other.

'A fellow can't be allowed to steal a child from a black mother, any more than from a white one,' she added, looking fixedly at Simon as she spoke.

'I hear these two have walked here from the station they call Balkara,' said a lean, brown-faced young man, who was on his way with a mob of cattle from the Lower Northern Territory. 'I am interested in them, for I heard of them on the way down.'

He had, in fact, got a letter from the man who, with his wife, had helped Iliapa on the way, by giving her some rations. In this letter was written: 'Do what you can, when you get to Labalama, for this poor mother who is going after her youngster. Simon is the sort of cad who would swear that black is white, for the sake of one old brown ha'penny.'

'Then they have come across some country where a snake cannot pick up a living this weather,' said an old bushman near him.

'I say, Simon, old man, you mustn't try to keep that fine little chap from his mother,' chimed in another man, going close up to the group, and looking at each in turn.

'Now, you people are yabbering a lot about a thing of which you know nothing whatsoever, nothing at all,' said Simon. 'I'm the last man that would try to do such a thing. Not only so, but if I saw anyone else trying on such a dirty trick, I would be the first to cry out against it. But there's more behind this than any of you know anything of. I'll explain it all at a proper time and place.'

There was something in Simon's tone and manner of speaking that imposed on most of those who heard him. He was indeed a very cunning creature, and finding that the people who gathered round him were quite on the side of the mother and her boy, he took aside two or three of the men, and whispered something to them, in which the words 'reputed father' and 'real father' played a part.

'Golly, do you really say that is true?' said the old bushman.

'I've heard of such things before,' said another.

But the young stockman laughed in Simon's face.

'That be hanged for a thin yarn of your spinning,' he said, as he walked away. He went back into the inn, but he stood by an open window, to see what would take place, set on helping the mother and boy as far as might be necessary.

One by one, the people who had gathered round went away, until only Iliapa, her boy, Polde and Simon were left. He now felt that he could not get rid of the two 'nigger women,' as he called them, without a good deal of trouble. He knew quite well that the law of the land would make him give up the lad to his mother. But he had had a good deal of practice in breaking the law of the land, and at the same time escaping punishment. He saw no reason why he should not do so this time also, with a little care. So he dropped the bullying tone, and the rough manner and said to Iliapa in a kindly sort of way:

'If you are really 'Baka's mother, I will, of course, give him up to you. But, you see, if I make a mistake, I may get myself into a great deal of trouble. This boy was given to me by one that had a right to him. . . .'

'He is not my father, I tell you that many times,' said Alibaka.

Then his mother joined in:

'All people know Yukuta not belong to us. Father to Alibaka away in Country of Great Salt Water, but him come back – p'raps soon.'

'He know quite well. This Simon one great big rogue. He tell 'um lie all the day, all the night, all the years,' said Polde in an undertone to Iliapa. Simon heard what she said, but it did not suit him to take any notice just then. So he went on, speaking in the same calm, one might say, kindly way:

'Well, but, you see, I only know what I am told. Yukuta tells me one thing, you tell me another. In this world, people do not always tell the truth.' Polde laughed out loud, but Simon took no notice, and went on:

'The thing for me is to get some proof that you are his mother, and that Yukuta had no right to the boy. In the first place, then, is there any white person in Labalama who knows that Alibaka belongs to you?'

'No, but Balkara Missus know, and Antaka people give 'um letter for Docker Grey, but Docker Grey, he big one bad in bed!' replied Iliapa.

'Oh, you have a letter have you?' said Simon, at once pricking up his ears at this bit of news. 'Then you had better let me see it, and read it, to see what is in it. This may be just the proof I want, at any rate as far as you are concerned.'

Iliapa hesitated, then raised her hand, as if to draw the letter out of her bosom. But Polde poked her sharply in the side, and said in the Arunta tongue:

'Don't be the 'possum that lay down on the fire to cook himself all over for eating.'

'Missus of Antaka say, me must give letter not to no one but to Docker,' said Iliapa. If a look could have killed anyone, then Polde must have curled up and died, under the glare of Simon's eyes. But he kept down his rage, and said to her half jokingly:

'What do you think I would do to the letter, then?'

'Put him in your pocket, and say you never see him; tear him in little bits; hold him in the candle till he come out black dust; stick him in your mouf and swallow him down your froat. You do a lot of fings to him, but you never give him safe back,' replied Polde, laughing, quite enjoying this chance of telling Simon in so many words that she knew he was a great rascal.

He walked a few steps away from the three, and having lit a fresh cigar, he came back to Iliapa and said in the tone of one who is more sorry than angry:

'As you will not let me read this letter you have, and as there is no one in Labalama who can be a witness for you, the only thing I can think of is to write to the Master and Missus at Balkara. If they write and say that this is your boy, well and good. You take him away from me the moment I get this proof, and later, proof that Yukuta has no right to Alibaka. You see, I want to do the just thing. I made a certain bargain with a man. I took his boy, so he said, mind you, so he said, and I promised to take care of him. One day, a strange black woman comes, and says to me, "This is my boy." I give the boy up to her. By-and-by the man comes with whom I made the bargain. "Where is my boy that you promised to take care of?" says he. I tell you that man might have me put into jail.'

'Big one good place for you, too, bestest place in the world for you,' said Polde, quite loud enough to be heard. But Simon did not let on that a word reached him.

'So you see how it is: until I get some proof that you are Alibaka's mother – and later about Yukuta – I must keep to my word. Let me see. The mail goes out the day after to-morrow. I'll write by that mail, and get an answer back in a little over three weeks. It is not long to wait, and you can see your boy – at least, you can see Alibaka, every day, except when we have to take little journeys away from the township. He is really as happy with me as the day is long. He rides about in the daytime and sleeps in the stable at night. It is time he was asleep now, for we have to be up early in the morning. Come, 'Baka, you had better say good-night to your friends.'

Iliapa drew her boy aside for a moment.

'My head is turning round. I do not know what I should do or say,' she whispered to him. 'But he cannot take you away from me now, can he? Oh, I would like to sleep near you to be sure you are safe.'

'No, no, no,' said Alibaka soothingly. 'It will be all right. He is as sure as I am that you are my mother. He got afraid, you see, when the other white people came round; he spoke to you quite softly. There are people here who will be kind and help us. Don't give that letter to anyone. The doctor may be better in two or three days. Good-night. You go to the camp with Aunt Nabata. We'll see each other again to-morrow morning.'

Iliapa strained her boy to her heart, but in spite of her, she could not keep the tears back. It had all turned out in such an upside-down way – so contrary to what she used to picture on that long journey. But Polde kept her spirits up.

'What you let the water blind your eyes for?' she said to Iliapa, speaking out loud, so as to be sure that Simon heard her. 'We want to sit down at this fine township for a bit, and we leave our boy here to-night, where he sleep near nice horses, that never steal or tell lies.'

Both Iliapa and 'Baka laughed a little at this thrust. But Polde was not satisfied without a more direct charge. When she got as far as the gate out of the yard, she turned and ran back to the stable door, at which Simon was standing, and said to him in a very distinct voice:

'Now, you take care. If you do one bit of bad to that good boy, you stole away like wild dog take 'em lamb, the good Queen of Inglan' an' of the Blacks will have your head chop' off like that,' and she made a mad swish with one finger across the other, as if she were slashing at a poisonous insect.

Simon raised the whip he held in his hand, as if to strike her. But in the twinkling of an eye she was beyond his reach, and cried out again, well within hearing distance:

'Don' you forget that, if you want to keep your very ugly red head wifout bein' chop' off!'

CHAPTER 27

Nabata was waiting for them at the mia-mia close to the fence. The rest of the blacks had gone some time before to the camps, that were half a mile away, on a branch of the Jerama.

'What did Simon say?' asked Nabata, as they started on the way. Iliapa was beginning to tell her, when they heard a low whistling behind them.

They turned to see the young stockman hurrying after them. He had been too far off to hear what was said, but he had seen through the open window, that the boy stayed with Simon, while the mother went away, and he wanted to tell her what she ought to do.

'You are the mother of the boy, are you not?' he said to Iliapa.

'Yes – Alibaka my own boy,' she replied in a trembling voice.

'Well, don't you let that man Simon stuff you with any of his lying yarns. The laws of this country will not let him keep your son. You go to the police trooper to-morrow, and tell him about your boy being stolen from you, and your coming all the way after him from Balkara. If the trooper is worth his salt, he will at once order Simon to give the boy to you.'

'Yes, and the good Queen of Inglan' an' of the Blacks will give him a hammerin' that he don' get over for a good bit,' said Polde in a joyous voice, proud to let the stockman see that she knew how the law of the country would be carried out.

'Right you are,' he replied with a laugh. Then he told them that he had to go away for nearly a week, and that if things did not turn out right, he would help them when he came back. With an exchange of 'Good nights' he went away back to the inn, and the three women went on their way.

Iliapa and Polde were delighted with the plan of getting the police trooper to help them. But Nabata, who knew that Simon and the trooper spent a great many of their evenings together in the bar-parlour of the Emu Inn, did not feel so sure that he would turn out to be much of a friend to them. However, she did not say much, but told them that the best time to see the trooper would be early in the morning, before he had left his house, which was near the doctor's place, not more than ten minutes' walk from the inn.

They were up so early next morning that they were half-way to the township when the sun arose, large and crimson, like a great ball of fire. Except on the Jerama side, where the trees and shrubs grew thick, and many birds and beasts lived, the country round Labalama was very bare, with low reddish-looking hills, rising out of a vast plain here and there – the plains and hills in many places strewn with gibber stones. The rising sun and the reddish earth between them, made a warm haze, as if thin flames, that could not be seen by the naked eye, spread all round.

'The sun will be so hot to-day – he will make water nearly boil at mid-day,' said Iliapa, who was thinking that, after all, it was a very good thing they were at the township, even though she had not yet got her boy away from Simon. As for Polde, she laughed and sang, and made up rhymes on the way, as if there were no such thing as any kind of trouble in all the wide world.

'Who is this I see coming to us, straight as a sapling of a stringy-bark gum, fast as a swan on the wing?' she chanted. 'Who but the son of Nalbuka and of Iliapa, the daughter of Erungara, the wise medicine man.' At first Iliapa thought that this was but a jest Polde was putting into rhyme. But soon she saw that Alibaka was really running towards them. Ah, what a joyful sight this was for her, and how fast she ran to meet him, and how much they had to say.

Alibaka had got up as early as his mother and Polde, and had seen to the horses, but when he knocked at Simon's door, Simon told him that he had changed his mind about getting away early, and that he need not saddle the horses till nine o'clock.

'When he said that, I came away to the camp, but here you are near the town.' His mother told him about going to see the trooper, but the boy seemed to be of the same opinion as his Aunt Nabata.

'I think,' he said, 'the trooper will only care for what Simon says to him. But when the doctor gets well, and reads the letter, then all will go straight. The doctor will know what to do.'

But though her sister and her son, who both knew so much more of the man than she did, had small hopes of what the police trooper would do in the cause of justice, yet Iliapa could not help hoping that he would do what was right. In this she was very likely a good deal moved by what Polde had so often said, of the 'good Queen of Inglan' an' of the Blacks' getting the law put into force by means of the police.

As a matter of fact, the police troopers in the remote parts of Australia are very often fine, good-hearted men, who do a great deal to keep things right, in places that are far away from the usual round of everyday life.

But the trooper who was then at Labalama was a man of very common clay, who cared chiefly for poor trashy things, such as drinking and betting, gossiping and playing cards for money, at the public-house, night after night, with Simon and other men of the same kind. Thus it was rather a hopeless thing, for poor Iliapa to go to him, to get her boy away from one of his most intimate friends. Simon had been careful to give him his own story of the affair on the evening before, after he had parted with Alibaka and his mother.

Iliapa had got but a little way in telling the trooper how she had come all the way from Balkara to get her boy, when he stopped her by saying roughly:

'It is no use you telling me a lot about yourself and your boy, without some proof that you are his mother. I will send for Mr Simon, and take down what he says.'

He did so, and in a short time Simon came into the little office in which Iliapa and Polde were waiting.

'You want to know how I came by the boy 'Baka?' he said to the trooper, who was sitting at the table, pen in hand, to write down what he said. This is his statement:

'The boy was given to me by his father, who could not feed him, nor clothe him – who could do nothing for him but leave him to die under a bush, like a dingo pup that has been knocked on the head. "I'll take him," says I, "I'll look after him, I'll teach him to ride, I'll give him plenty of tucker three times a day, I'll give him clothes to wear and a horse to ride. But mind you this, if I do all this for him, you must promise me one thing." "What is that?" says Yukuta. "You must promise that you will give him up to me altogether – altogether, mind you," says I, "so that after I've trained him, fed him, clothed him, looked after him like a father in every way, you'll not come loafing after him, or try to take him away." "I promise you I will never come near him, or try to take him away," says Yukuta. And, mind you, Yukuta has kept his word. He may be a bit of a scoundrel – mind you, I don't say he isn't. But he has kept his word.'

Nothing broke the silence in the trooper's office as he wrote Simon's statement on an official sheet of paper. A student of human nature might find some interest in this document. Here was a damaged and damaging man without a rag to cover his moral nakedness, fighting to tear a boy from his mother to keep him in a state of abject slavery. Yet in the action picturing himself as a bulwark for the destitute and the forsaken – a just man overflowing with the milk of human kindness.

His tissue of brazen lies filled Iliapa with sickening fear. She had never forgotten how Nalbuka had been put into jail for 'killing a cow he had never seen.' She knew, too, from words spoken by her father when his mind wandered for some days before he died, that it was the danger of being charged with a crime he had not committed that made Nalbuka flee to a far country and stay away so long that it often seemed as if she would never see him again. Thus, in a vague way, the law of the land looked to her like some wild force of nature – like a flood or a hurricane or a thunderbolt – that may at times smite down the guiltless and leave the guilty untouched. The passion with which she had turned on Yukuta for his cruelty to her father failed her now. She was too much worn with fatigue and anxiety and the dread that her boy might, after all, be kept from her. She shivered now and then as if from cold, and the tears streamed down her face unchecked.

But Polde was in a very different state of mind. The many vivid stories and pictures that had been shown and read to her when she was a little girl by the children of Moorano at the time of Queen Victoria's first Jubilee were always fresh in her memory, and always gave her the feeling that she and all black people were under the care and regard of the British crown, and that the police were given their bread and their stripes to do just as much for them as for the whites. Before they came into the trooper's office, Iliapa had strongly warned her not to get heated, not to be 'cheeky' or speak loud or get angry at anything that might take place. By a great effort she had kept still while Simon spoke and while the trooper wrote. When he had done and said in a pompous way, 'Now I am ready to hear the other side,' Polde at once stepped forward.

'But you are not the mother,' said Simon, who shrank from the set face and the flashing eyes that fronted him.

'An' you don' be the mas'er trooper of the good Queen of Inglan' an' of the Blacks,' replied Polde, making up for the calmness of her speech by a look of flaming scorn. 'You see, Mas'er Trooper,' she went on in a placidly polite voice, 'my mate, Iliapa, she don' be able to speak good. She trem'le like a bird cotched in a net, an' she cry an' her head go roun' for the drefful lies she hear. You 'low me talk for her.'

'Yes, you may give your evidence. But what do you mean by dreadful lies?'

'All them words you scrat down on that paper is a big one boomer lie. Simon giv'um Yukuta gun, sharp nipe, heap twobaccy for tell him where he meet Alibaka alone. Simon meet the fine boy of Iliapa that was always pet at Balkara, wear'um nice cloes, top boots shine like lookum glass, plenty of good tucker all the times, ride fast horse for mas'er of Balkara. Simon say to him, 'Your father, Nalbuka, big one sick, he want you. I have horse for you to ride, this one go back to Balkara.' Alibaka, he good boy, he don' know Simon was a teremenjious liar an' want to steal him away like wild dingo dog take'um poor little lamb. . . . '

'Be careful what you say,' warned the trooper, but giving Simon a sidelong look of mingled inquiry and mistrust.

Simon met the glance with the air of one whose moral feelings have been dealt a severe blow. 'Of all the made-up tales that ever I heard – this beats them hollow. I never thought that even a nigger-woman would invent such a yarn.' He spoke in a low tone, meant only for the trooper's ears. But Polde's hearing was acute and she at once made answer. 'Don' you call me nack-name. Me black woman – you be white rascal nigger. You go an' brang that boy back to his mother. You be trooper for the good Queen of Inglan' an' of the Blacks,' she turned as she spoke to the trooper, holding up her hand to give more force to her words. 'Tell him to once, "Give that boy you stealed back to his mother and to her mate Polde, what come all the way for him to Labalama."'

'Do you dare to give me orders what I should do?' cried the trooper, his vanity deeply wounded by Polde's tone of command.

'All people know Alibaka my boy; Polde say true,' chimed in Iliapa, who by this time had wiped her tears away, and got back her courage.

'I will hear you now,' said the trooper. 'As for you,' turning to Polde, 'I have heard as much as I want to of your tongue; you may go away.'

'Yes, me go,' said Polde, turning to the door. But it had been hard for her to keep her temper within bounds. What rankled most was seeing Simon's tale gravely put on paper. Standing by the open door, she now made a comment on that event. 'You got'um big one silly cocoa-nut on you to scrat down on paper what that boy-stoler Simon tole you. He make you one big jackass. An' if. . . . '

'If you say another word, I'll have you put in the lock-up,' roared the trooper, coming to the door with a face full of menace. Polde gave a shrill war-cry and ran out of sight. But no sooner had the trooper taken his seat and begun to question Iliapa, than Polde put her head in at the door and called out, 'If you don't stop drinking' grogs at night with Simon, the good Queen of Inglan' an' of the Blacks, she pull off your jacke' an' your grousers with the strips an' send you to crack stones to men' the roads.'

The last part of the warning was shouted from a distance, Polde running away with the strides of an emu, while the trooper stood at the door, his face aflame with rage, and partly, no doubt, the effects of the 'grogs' thus shouted as it were from the house-tops.

Simon thought all this was water for his mill. His face showed the pleasure he got from the turn affairs had taken. But the trooper, though a foolish man and lacking all dignity of character, had not passed his fortieth year without learning a little of the world in which he lived.

He heard Iliapa with more kindness than he had first shown. At the end he gave a promise that she should see Alibaka part of each day until a letter came from the Master of Balkara.

This promise lifted a weight from Iliapa's mind. 'You see, Polde, Simon cannot take him away now,' she said as the two sat talking together that night in their mia-mia at the native women's camp. 'Missus will write at once; then the three of us will go back together, after the worst part of the summer is over. Perhaps Nalbuka will be back at Balkara before we get there.'

CHAPTER 28

Five days passed quickly, Iliapa seeing her boy for some time daily. She began feeling sure of getting him away from Simon, as soon as Dr Grey recovered, or at latest when a letter should come from Balkara.

On the sixth day after she had come, Alibaka went with Simon to some races at Yarana. They did not come back until late on the next day, and as soon as Iliapa set eyes on her boy, she saw that he had been hurt. There was an ugly bruise on the left brow, and a swelling round both his eyes.

At first, he tried to hide from her what had taken place. But after she had been talking with him alone for some time, he told her that Simon had struck him with the butt-end of his whip. He got into a rage because one of his horses had lost a race. He blamed Alibaka for this, and when the boy said it was not his fault, and that the horse was a poor beast, the wretched coward struck him in this cruel way.

Afterwards he made Alibaka promise that he would tell no one, said he was sorry he hurt him, and that he would not do so any more. All the old fears came crowding into Iliapa's mind.

'He may kill him, or do something bad to him, if I do not get him away at once,' she thought to herself, as she listened and looked at the big swollen bruise on her boy's face. The two were sitting on a rough bench that stood close to the stable. While Iliapa sat without a word, thinking of one plan after another for getting Alibaka away from the horrible man who had him in his power, Polde came running up, crying out in her loud cheerful voice, 'Here you are. I been looking for you everywhere, long time. Nabata. . . . ' Here Polde stopped short, for though the twilight was closing in, her sharp eyes caught sight of the bruise and the swelling round Alibaka's eyes.

She took the boy's face between her hands and looked into his eyes, and said in a shrill voice:

'Tell me what hurt you.'

Alibaka said nothing, and made a sign to his mother not to tell, for he was afraid of rousing Polde's violent anger. But keeping silence did no good; she at once guessed the truth.

'It was Simon, it was Simon. You came at once to the young Docker and show him what that wicket beast-man do to you boy,' she said to Iliapa in a tone of authority. Questioning Alibaka she found out how he had been struck.

'You never, never go near Simon any more,' she said, while the tears streamed down her cheeks. Then dashing them away, she ran to the stable and came back with a thick strong whip that she saw in a vehicle at the door.

'If we meet him on the way, that is what he will get very quick and very heavy on his very ugly fat face, and his very ugly red head.' Polde as she spoke waved the whip with as much vigour as if the enemy stood within reach. She was so deeply moved by the old tribal instinct for revenge, that Iliapa rose in terror at the sound of footsteps drawing near.

It was the young stockman who had returned from a station sixty miles away where he had been settling up about some stock he had brought from the Lower Northern Territory.

'So you are here, all three – I want to have some talk with you,' he said. But it was Polde's turn first. She told of their visit to the trooper's office and how he failed them in making Simon give up the boy.

'An' now see what the animal-man doned to-day wif the heaby en' of his whipt.'

She encircled Alibaka's face with her slender hands and drew it forward, so that it should be clearly seen. The young man's face burned as he looked at the boy's bruised and swollen face.

'You three stay here till I come back. I know where to find that. . . . ' He coupled some words with Simon's name that were as sweet to Polde as wild honey-comb. When he had gone a few yards, he turned back to ask, 'What is the name of the boy's father?' 'Nalbuka, Nalbuka, Nalbuka,' they all cried in chorus. 'Ah, that's good – I have grand bit of news to tell you when I get back.'

When he got to the inn and asked for James Simon, the landlady showed him into a parlour where he sat with the police trooper at a table adorned with all the items needed for the 'grogs' of which Polde had spoken with so little reserve.

'It is you I came to see,' said the stockman, addressing Simon. 'But since your friend is here, I will ask him a question. You are a policeman; you stand for law and order. What do you think a fellow deserves who steals a boy from his mother and refuses to give him up after she has followed him on foot for two hundred miles, over some of the worst country in Australia?'

'It is my duty to consider matters from a legal point of view – not to be carried away by the floating gossip of an out-back place like this,' returned the trooper with a very pompous air, edging away by degrees from Simon and the tell-tale table, as if they were part of the floating gossip with which he had little or nothing to do.

'And if the thief strikes the boy in the face brutally with the butt-end of a whip – what then?'

'Is it a riddle you are putting to me?' asked the trooper, but with a look at his boon companion full of inquiry. Simon, on his part, tried hard to put on the look of a just man whose good name is made the prey of wicked tongues, making fine use of the trooper's lead as to the endless lying tales that are part and parcel of Bush townships, but more marked and to an extent not to be told in a place like Labalama.

The stockman looked from one man to the other, each with a red face deeply flushed, padded with fat, and said, more as if thinking aloud than speaking to anyone:

'Birds of a feather!'

'What am I to understand by that?' said the trooper, now holding himself very erect, almost with his back to Simon and the table with its bottles and siphon and half-filled glasses.

'Part of an old saying – nearly as true as the endless gossip is sometimes. To put it more plainly – it strikes me that you are up to the neck in a very dirty job.' Turning to Simon, he said, 'I came to give you a sound thrashing for treating a helpless boy like the cowardly bully you are. But you are soaked and sodden with drink – it would turn my stomach to touch you. Only mind this: you are never to go near that boy again, or have anything to do with him. He is in my charge till his *father* comes.'

As soon as he got back to the little group on the bench, he told them the 'grand bit of news.' On his way from Pallapallama, he came on the mail-coach that ran every three weeks between Labalama and Erguma. One of the wheels had got badly damaged. The driver and three passengers were by the track trying to mend it up as best they could. He had some straps that he gave them, and they patched up the break so that they would be able to reach Labalama to-morrow morning. One of the passengers was a black man who had come all the way from the Northern Territory. He heard the driver call him Nalbuka.

'That is father,' cried Alibaka. 'He be coming. Oh, he be coming,' said Polde with a little shriek as of victory. 'You yabber along a him?' asked Iliapa, in the timid voice of one who fears to make too sure of a great joy.

'No. But as I was riding along I began to wonder who the black man could be that was coming in such haste to Labalama. It was like a dream to me that one of you told me Alibaka's father was in the Country of the Great Salt Water. Somehow I began to think it was your father.' He put his hand on Alibaka's shoulder as he spoke. 'Now the name makes it certain.'

'We go a bit on – camp near 'um track an' meet Nalbuka early morning; no can stop longer.' Iliapa as she spoke rose with the movement of one going to run a race. She had waited so many years – she could wait no longer. Her impulse met with a quick response.

'The very best thing you could do,' said the stockman, thinking of the little mob that would crowd round the coach full of idle curiosity at the meeting of the long-parted family. 'Oh, we go – we go this moment,' cried Alibaka, clapping his hands. As for Polde, laughing brokenly, while the tears ran down her cheeks, she ran to tell Nabata, and to gather up the few things they would want for their joyful little trek.

A little after they started the stockman came running after them with a packet of dates and biscuits he had bought in the general store, that was close to the inn. 'I will be on the look-out for you,' he said, 'after the coach comes in to-morrow.'

'Oh, you big one good,' cried Polde in her loud frank voice, while Iliapa and her boy gave thanks in a shyer fashion.

'Now I tell you some poemry the good chil'en of Moorano telled me when I was pickaninny,' and forthwith Polde half-chanted the lines:

> The black mand an' the white –
> Boff have a claim on life,
> An' if they boff do right
> There is no cause for strife.

'Good,' said the stockman, laughing. 'We must write that on a ticket and tie it round Simon's neck.'

'Yes, tie 'um a bid tight till he be like a fat frog squimbjiling in the mouf of a kookaburra,' cried Polde in a gleeful voice.

The old moon that had seen Iliapa and her mate through their long journey had faded out of the world; the baby moon newly born had set. But it was a lovely night, warm and still, with a wonderful limpid sky filled to the brim with stars. They camped by a group of salt-bushes well within sight of the track by which the mail-coach would come. They were so much excited, they felt it was useless to think of sleeping for some time. Polde told of a great corroboree she had seen long ago when she was a small child. The men gave much meat to the women and the women gave them pitchies full of manna they had gathered from the gum-trees. Then Iliapa told one of her Aunt Labea's tales about a bell-bird that sent two painted finches to an old medicine man who was all alone under a wattle-tree. Then she chanted the song of the bell-bird:

Baku baku wa yan thidna
Win Maru
Win mure baku bakungu.

Polde joined in and told how a crow who had nothing to eat for three days but one witchetty-grub and half a sugar-bag, got so cross when he heard the bell-bird singing, that he cried out, 'Keep quiet, or I will put you in a hole in the ground, and sit down on top of it.'

At last, one by one they fell asleep.

Iliapa was the first to awake. It was just at the break of dawn. With the blacks, this is a favourite moment for many of their more important and sacred ceremonies. Also for setting out on long journeys. This may be the reason why so many of their tales of the long-ago begin with the words: 'It was when the dawn began to make the sky red.' This made Iliapa think. What a fine moment for the mail-coach to come into sight! But this did not happen till an hour after sunrise. They had made some tea, and were eating biscuits and dates, when all at once Iliapa got up, and ran some little distance along the track. Yes, there was the sound of a trap in the distance. It was a slow lumbering sound that carried far, but at last it came in sight. Memories of his old plans for going to meet his father alone must have come into Alibaka's mind. For the moment the coach came into view, he said: 'Nandi, you stay here with Polde; let me go to Batja alone.'

Iliapa, of course, agreed. She and Polde watched the boy fly like a bird on the wing till he got close to the trap, saw Nalbuka jump out of it and hold his son in his arms, as if he would never let him go. Polde wept and laughed aloud at the sight: Iliapa was silent, but tears of joy gathered in her eyes. At last all her fears were over, and the cup of her happiness was full.

PANDORA PRESS

Pandora Press is a feminist press, an imprint of Routledge & Kegan Paul. Our list is varied – we publish new fiction, reprint fiction, history, biography and autobiography, social issues, humour – written by women and celebrating the lives and achievements of women the world over. For further information about Pandora Press books, please write to the Mailing List Dept. at Pandora Press, c/o Methuen Law Book Co., 44 Waterloo Road, North Ryde, NSW 2113, Australia or in London at 11 New Fetter Lane, London EC4P 4EE.

Some Pandora titles you will enjoy ►

ORANGES ARE NOT THE ONLY FRUIT

Jeanette Winterson

'Like most people I lived for a long time with my mother and father. My father liked to watch the wrestling, my mother liked to wrestle. . .'

'The achievement of this novel is to make us squirm with laughter, then make us acknowledge how utterly sad it is when the needs of self-preservation turn what has been sacred into a joke.'

Roz Kaveney, *Times Literary Supplement*

'*Oranges* is a brilliant first novel – at once witty, gripping, imaginative and touching.'

Time Out

Paper Fiction 086358 042 4
Winner of the 1985 Publishing for People Prize for First Novel

THIS PLACE

Andrea Freud Loewenstein

'An energetic and passionate novel which grips the reader's attention with unholy force. It is an extraordinary evocation of a closed world – female bodies and female minds struggling against an imprisonment equally dire whether enforced or self-imposed, and written with charity and understanding.'

Fay Weldon

'Loewenstein vividly creates, through a naturalistic fidelity to voice and description, a stifling inferno.'

Michele Roberts

Cloth Fiction 086358 039 4
Paper 086358 040 8

CHARLEYHORSE

Cecil Dawkins

This is an explosive gallop through the family fortunes of mother and daughter on their huge ranch in Kansas.

Mother is a megalomaniac, daughter as stubborn as the bulls she manages; Cecil Dawkins' novel reworks traditional Western themes and is guaranteed to make you laugh, cry and see red.

Cecil Dawkins lives in New Mexico.

Cloth Fiction 086358 096 3
Pandora edition not available in USA or Canada

NATURAL SELECTION

Margaret Mulvihill

Maureen works as a slave in a London publishing house and lives on the borders of literary London. Life is a series of groggy mornings, tedious days working on other people's manuscripts and planning illicit meetings with Martin. Until a certain manuscript falls mysteriously into her hands. . .

This witty novel describes a publishing world filled with sex, adultery, plagiarism, opportunism . . . as well as books.

To be read in the bath while eating expensive chocolates.

Cloth Fiction 086358 064 5
Paper 086358 058 0

A WOMAN CALLED EN

Tomie Ōhara

Written by a major modern Japanese novelist, this book won two major literary awards on its publication in Japan.

Based on fact, the novel is set in seventeenth century Japan and centres round En who at four years old is confined with her family to a single house, isolated from society and human contact, when her father falls from political favour. There she remains for forty years but she prevails, strong and refusing to be defeated.

Written in the formal classical style of the seventeenth century, this novel is nevertheless a modern novel, movingly written and painfully felt.

Cloth Fiction 086358 079 3
Paper 086358 082 3

LITTLE TOURS OF HELL

Tall Tales of Food and Holidays

Josephine Saxton

Painting holidays, pregnant holidays, ghastly weekends and reckless rendezvous . . . these are just a few Saxton scenarios to help you get away from it all, with these cautionary tales about campers, hampers and oily foreign muck for gastronomiques and holiday makers everywhere.

These stories are specifically concerned with the more macabre or stultifying aspects of eating and holidaying. Josephine Saxton is able to unravel the disturbing implications behind the most innocent and everyday activities with an acute and very witty eye for detail in sharp and brilliant prose.

Cloth Fiction 086358 094 7 176pp
Paper 086358 095 5

STEPPING OUT

Edited by Ann Oosthuizen

This imaginative collection of short stories celebrates friendship between women and explores the new lives that women are leading today. The stories range from love stories to friendships and betrayals, to the relationship between sisters and women in conflict with contributions from
Anna Livia
Honora Bartlett
Barbara Burford
Michelene Wandor
Ann Oosthuizen
Marsha Rowe
Jackie Kay
Moy McCrory
Andrea Loewenstein
Jo Jones
Sara Maitland

Paper Fiction 086358 488 3 176pp

PASSION FRUIT

Romantic Fiction with a Twist

Edited by Jeanette Winterson

A collection of short romances which adds a new and startling dimension to the traditional scenario of love, lust and marriage with stories from:
Rebecca Brown
Angela Carter
Laurie Colwin
Fiona Cooper
Sara Maitland
Bobby Ann Mason
Marge Piercy
Josephine Saxton
Aileen La Tourette
Lorna Tracey
Michelene Wandor
Fay Weldon

Paper Fiction 086358 070 X 200pp

AUTOBIOGRAPHY OF A CHINESE GIRL

Hsieh Ping-Ying

With an introduction by Elisabeth Croll

This is the story of Hsieh Ping-Ying, a Chinese girl born at the beginning of this century who rejected the traditions of the old order and eventually became one of China's leading women writers.

At school, she unwrapped the binding on her feet so that she could run freely with the other children. As a young woman she went into the army in order to escape an arranged marriage. As an adult she was charged with being a communist and imprisoned.

Hsieh Ping-Ying's story takes us back to the heart of pre-revolutionary China. She describes her relationship with her family: with her mother and with her grandmother and the difficulties she faced rejecting traditional constraints in order to live as an independent woman.

Paper Autobiography 086358 052 1
244p